My First Dictionary

나만의
원어민 친구
Saypen

WorldCom Edu

How to Use Your Dictionary

The words in the dictionary are listed in A-B-C order. The dictionary shows how to spell words, what words mean, and how words change form. Each word has a full-color photo to show what it means. These lively photos help to engage children's interest. The guide words at the top of the page make it easy to find the words you are looking for in the dictionary.

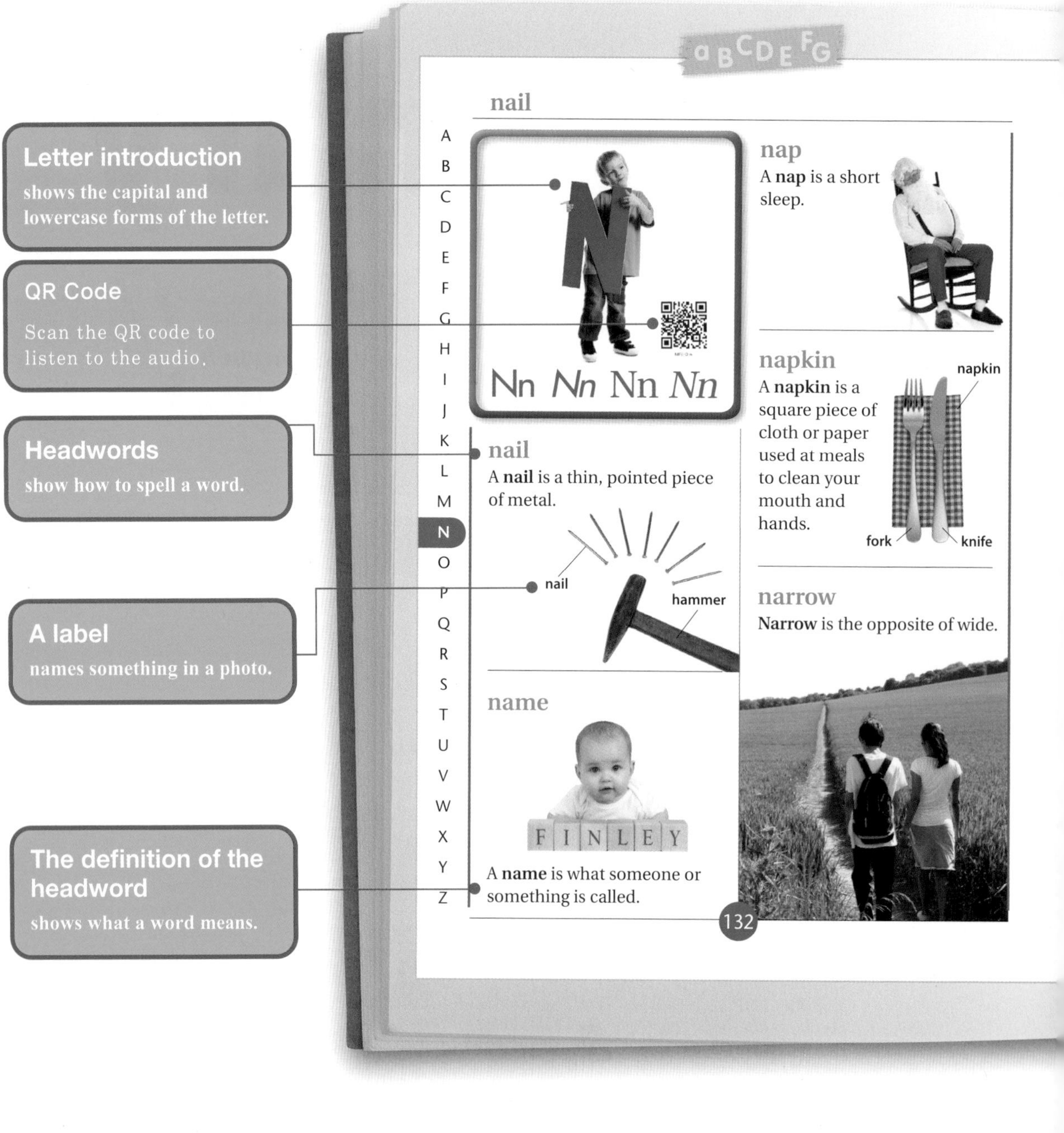

needle

nature
People, animals, plants, sky, land, and water are all parts of **nature**.

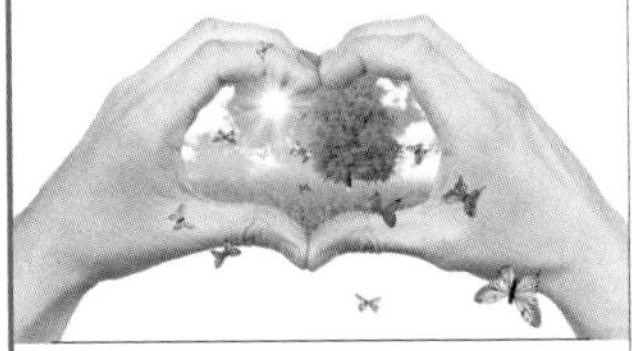

navy · navies
A **navy** is all the warships of a country.

near
Near means being close to something or someone.

neat

Neat means clean and tidy.

neck
The **neck** is the part of the body between the head and the shoulders.

needle
A **needle** is a thin, sharp-pointed tool for sewing.

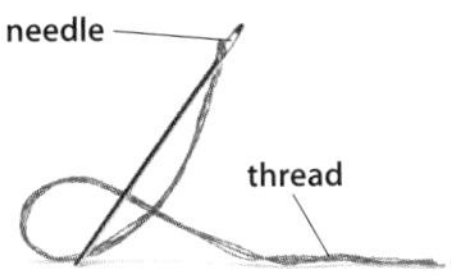

a b c d e f g h i j k l m **n** o p q r s t u v w x y z

133

Guide words
show the first or the last word on the page.

Alternative forms of headwords
show how some headwords change into other forms.

Alphabet bar
shows which letter of the alphabet you are looking at.

Photos
illustrate the word and help make the meaning clear.

How to Use Your Saypen

All Words & Meanings
If you click on Letter Introduction with your saypen, you can hear all words starting with the introduced letter and their meanings.

Word in the Image
If you choose each word in the image, you can hear the word.

Word Definition
If you click on the sentence, you can hear the word's meaning.

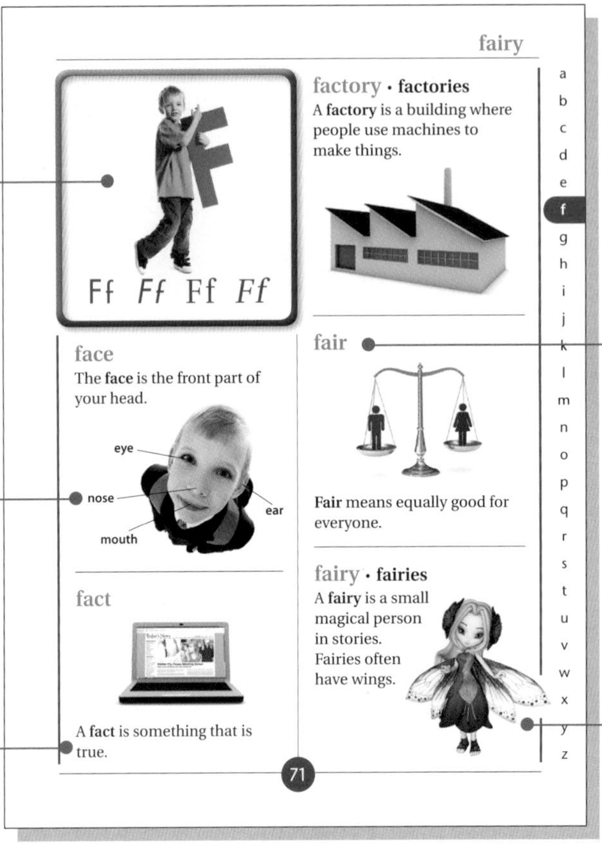

Word
If you choose the word with your saypen, you can hear the word spoken by the native speaker.

Image
If you click on the image, you can hear the word and its meaning .

- ☑ My Own Native Friend
- ☑ A Fun Way to Learn English Words
- ☑ Pronunciation Training through Saypen's Repeat Mode

Download MP3 files to Saypen

WorldCom Homepage (www.wcbooks.co.kr)

Contents

A 6
B 17
C 33
D 51
E 62
F 71
G 86
H 93
I 105
J 108
K 110
L 113
M 123
N 132
O 138
P 142
Q 161
R 163
S 171
T 194
U 207
V 210
W 212
X 220
Y 221
Z 223
A
B

absent

If you are **absent** from a place, you are not there.

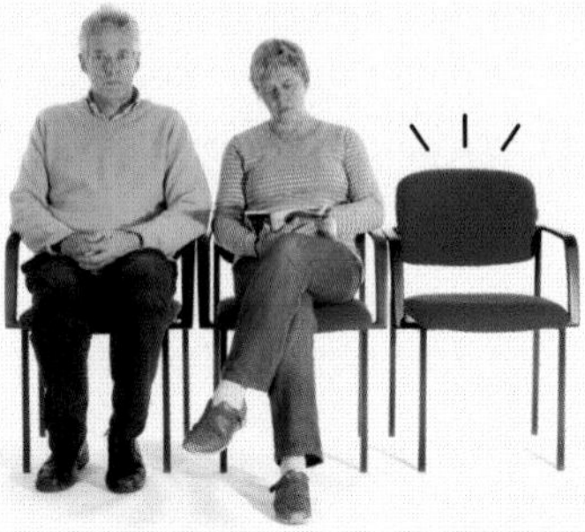

accident

An **accident** is something that happens suddenly, usually bad.

above

Above means higher than or over.

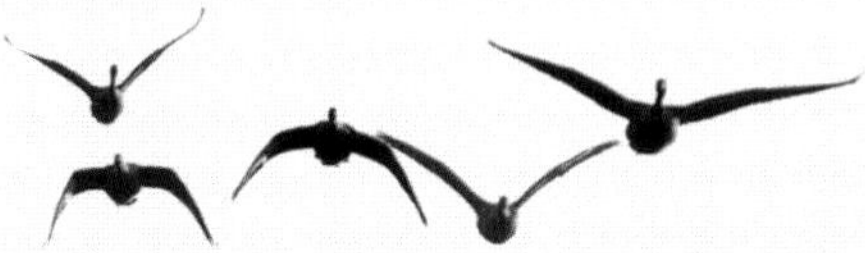

ache

An **ache** is a pain in your body that goes on hurting, like a **neckache**.

acorn

An **acorn** is the small brown nut that is the fruit of an oak tree.

across

Across means on the opposite side of something.

act

Act means to pretend to be someone else or to be in a play or movie.

add

Add means to put things together.

address

An **address** tells people where a place is, so they can go there or send mail there.

adult

An **adult** is a fully grown person.

A B C D E F G H I J K L M N O P Q R S T U V W X Y Z

afraid

When you feel **afraid**, you are frightened.

afternoon

Afternoon is the time between noon and evening.

again

Again means one more time.

age

Your **age** is the number of years you have lived.

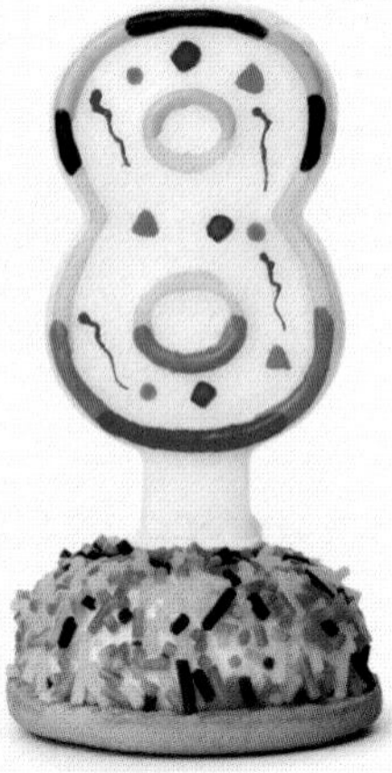

agree

Agree means to think the same as other people.

ahead

Ahead means in front of something.

air

We breathe **air**. It is all around us, and birds and aircraft fly in it.

air conditioner

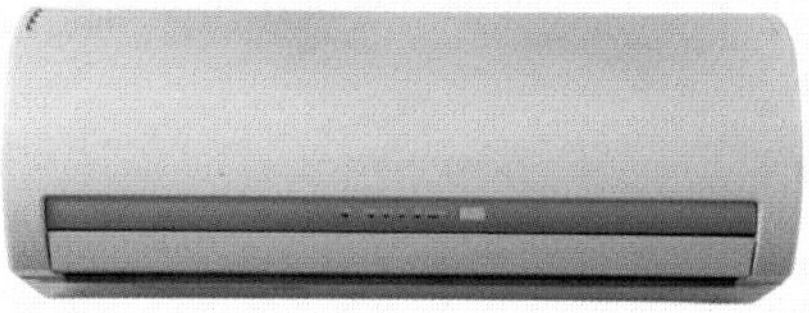

An **air conditioner** is a machine that cools and dries air.

airplane

An **airplane** is a flying vehicle with wings and engines.

airport

An **airport** is a place where airplanes take off and land.

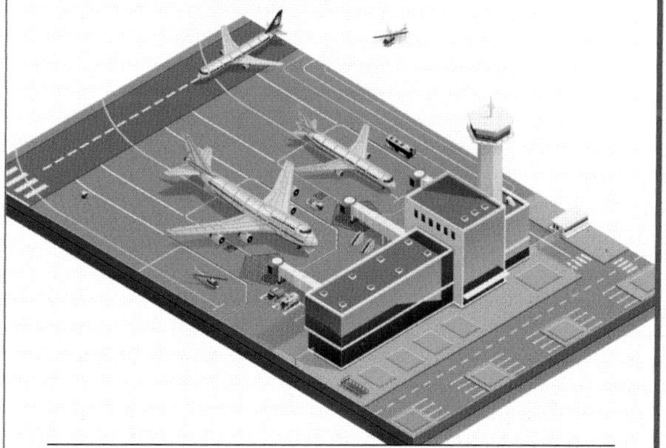

alarm

An **alarm** is a device to warn you of danger or to wake you up.

album

An **album** is a book in which you keep photographs.

alike

Things that are **alike** are almost the same.

alive

Alive means not dead.

all

All means every one or every part of something.

alligator

An **alligator** is an animal which has a long tail, short legs and a large mouth.

alone

When you are **alone**, you are not with anybody else.

along
Along means from one end to the other end.

alphabet
The **alphabet** is the letters we use to write words.

always

Always means every time or all the time.

amazing
Amazing means very surprising.

ambulance
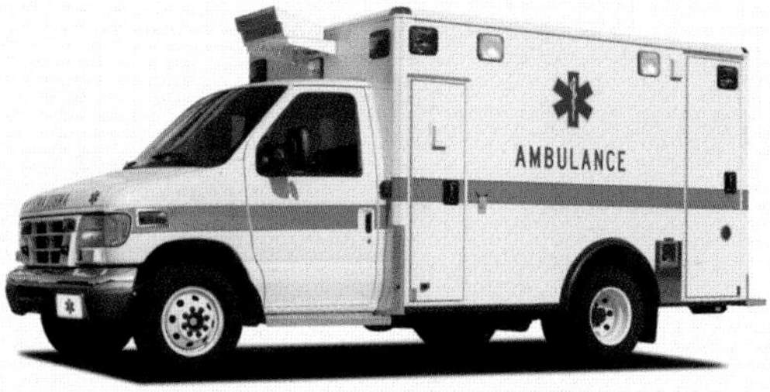

Ambulances are used to carry injured or sick people to a hospital.

anchor
An **anchor** is a large, metal hook on a long chain.

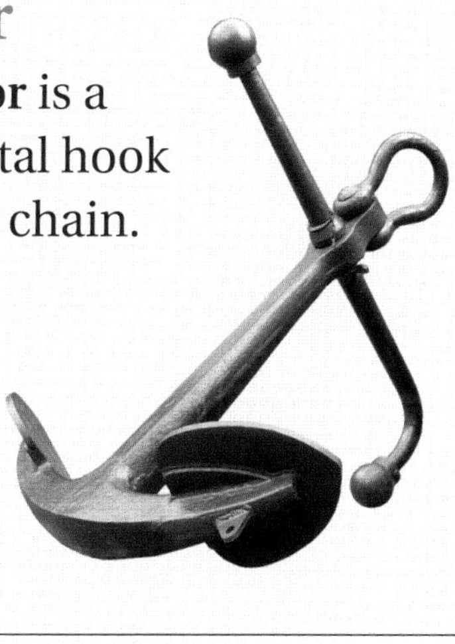

a b c d e f g h i j k l m n o p q r s t u v w x y z

ancient

Ancient means belonging to the distant past.

angry

If somebody is **angry**, they are mad.

animal

An **animal** is any living thing except a plant or a human.

ankle

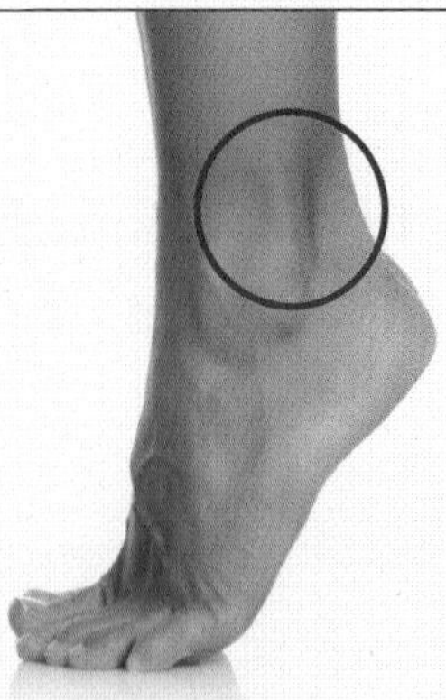

Your **ankle** is the part of your body where your foot joins your leg.

answer

Answer means to reply to someone's question or statement.

ant

An **ant** is a small insect that lives in the ground.

apart

Apart means away from each other.

ape

An **ape** looks like a large monkey without a tail.

apologize

Apologize means to say that you are sorry.

apple

An **apple** is a round fruit with a green, red, or yellow skin.

apron

An **apron** is a cloth which you wear to keep clean.

arm

An **arm** is the part of the body between the shoulder and the hand.

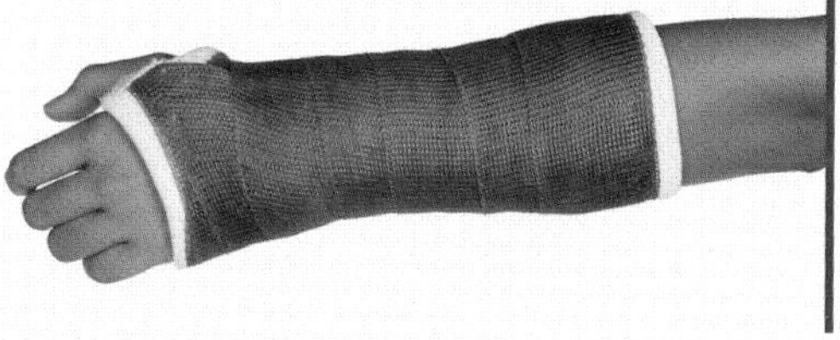

around

Around means on all sides of something or someone.

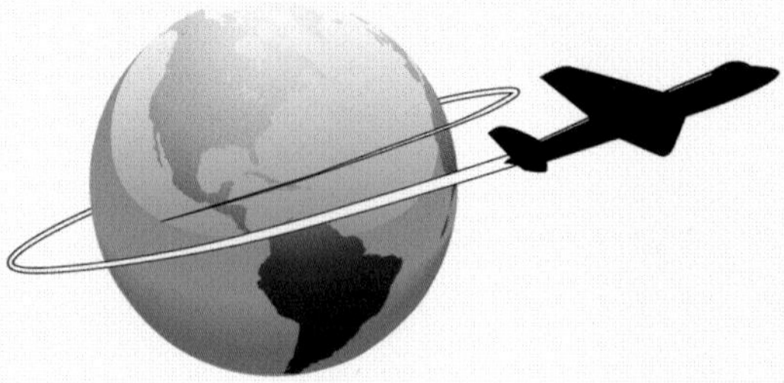

arrest

Arrest means to take somebody to a police station.

arrow

An **arrow** is a sign that points to show direction.

art

Art is something beautiful that somebody has made, like a painting or a statue.

artist

An **artist** is a person who makes beautiful things like paintings or drawings.

ash • ashes

Ash is the grey or black powder left after something has been burned.

ask

Ask means to give a question.

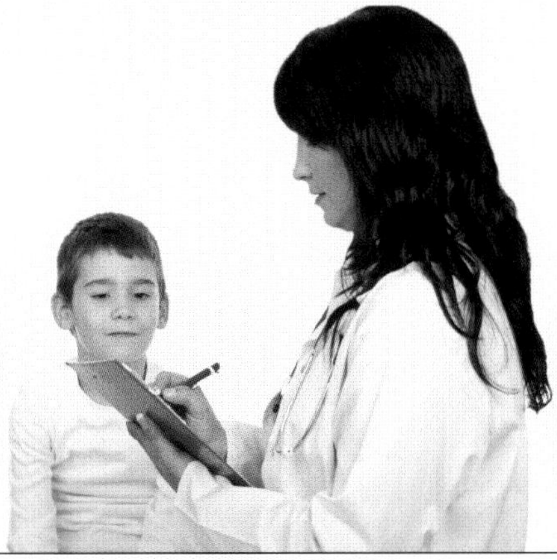

asleep

Asleep means sleeping.

astronaut

An **astronaut** is a person who travels in space.

athlete

An **athlete** is a person who is good at sports.

aunt

An **aunt** means the sister of one of your parents, or the wife of your uncle.

a b c d e f g h i j k l m n o p q r s t u v w x y z

A
B
C
D
E
F
G
H
I
J
K
L
M
N
O
P
Q
R
S
T
U
V
W
X
Y
Z

automobile

An **automobile** is a car.

autumn

Autumn is the part of the year that comes after summer.

awake

When you are **awake**, you are not asleep.

away

Away means not near.

ax • **axes**

An **ax** is a tool with a long handle and a sharp blade.

MFE-D-b

Bb Bb Bb Bb

baby • babies
A **baby** is a very young child.

back
A **back** is the part of the body behind the chest.

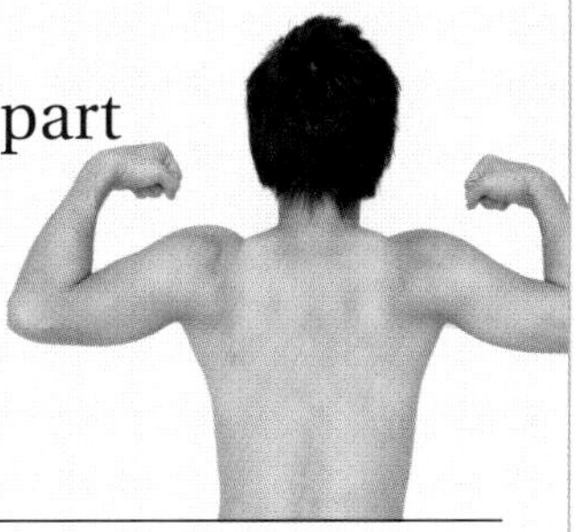

bacon

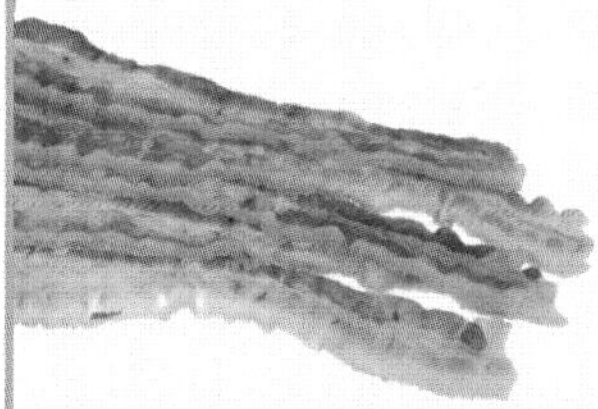

Bacon is meat from a pig's belly.

bad
Bad means not good.

bag

People use **bags** to carry things.

bake
Bake means to cook food in an oven.

balance

When you **balance**, you keep steady without falling.

ball

A **ball** is a round thing that you use in games.

balloon

A **balloon** is a bag filled with air or gas.

banana

A **banana** is a long fruit with a yellow skin.

band

A **band** is a group of people who play music together.

bank

A **bank** is a place to save money.

barber

A **barber** is a person whose job is to cut men's hair.

bark

When a dog **barks**, it makes a loud sound.

baseball

Baseball is a game played with a bat and a ball.

basket

A **basket** is used to hold things. It is usually made of wood or straw.

basketball

Basketball is a game played by two teams with a large ball.

bat

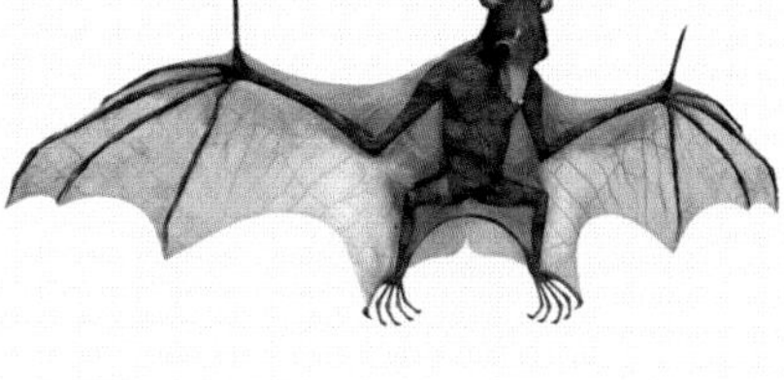

A **bat** is an animal like a mouse with wings.

A
B
C
D
E
F
G
H
I
J
K
L
M
N
O
P
Q
R
S
T
U
V
W
X
Y
Z

bath

A **bath** is washing your body with water.

bear

A **bear** is a large animal with brown, black, or white fur.

beach • **beaches**

A **beach** is an area of sand next to the sea.

beard

A **beard** is the hair that grows on a man's chin and cheeks.

bean

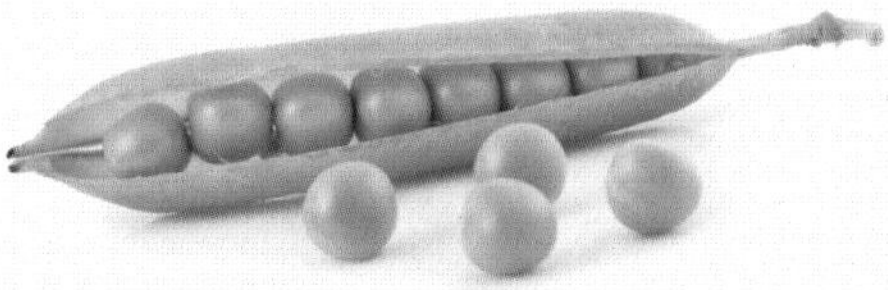

A **bean** is the seed of a plant that can be cooked and eaten.

beat • **beat, beaten**

Beat means to hit something again and again.

beautiful

Beautiful means very pretty to look at.

bed

A **bed** is a thing to sleep on.

beaver

A **beaver** is an animal with a wide tail and large teeth.

bee

A **bee** is a flying insect that makes honey.

become • became, become

Become means to change into something.

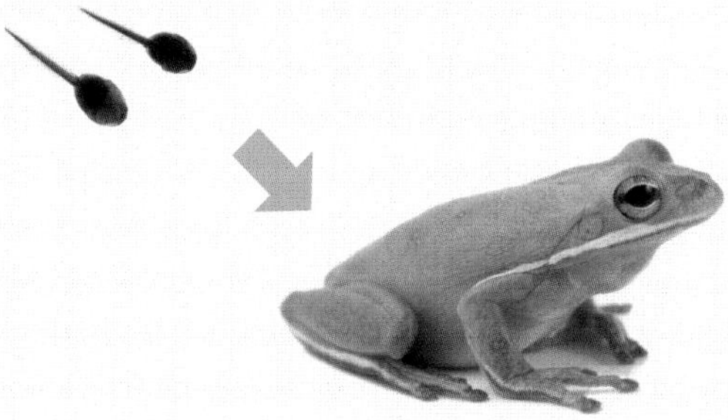

beggar

A **beggar** is a person who lives by asking people for money or food.

A
B
C
D
E
F
G
H
I
J
K
L
M
N
O
P
Q
R
S
T
U
V
W
X
Y
Z

behind

Behind means at the back of something.

believe

Believe means to think that something is true.

bell

A **bell** is an object or device which makes a ringing sound.

below

Below means under.

belt

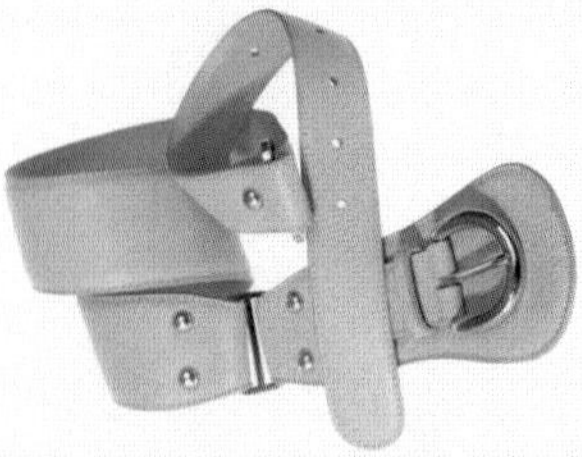

A **belt** is a piece of cloth or leather that you wear around your waist.

bench • **benches**

A **bench** is a long seat for two or more people.

bend • **bent**

If you **bend** something, it is not straight anymore.

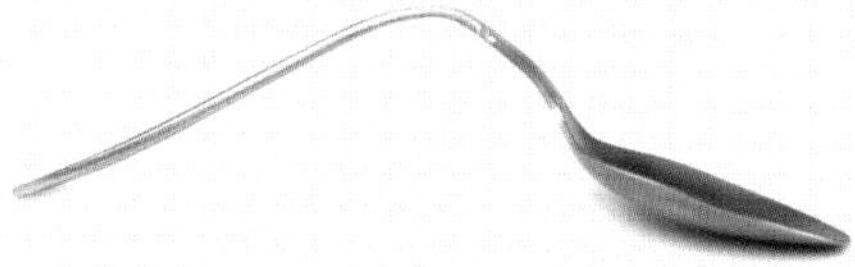

beside

Beside means next to something.

between

Between means in the middle of two things.

Bible

The **Bible** is a book that talks about God.

bicycle

A **bicycle** is something with wheels and pedals which people ride.

A
B
C
D
E
F
G
H
I
J
K
L
M
N
O
P
Q
R
S
T
U
V
W
X
Y
Z

big

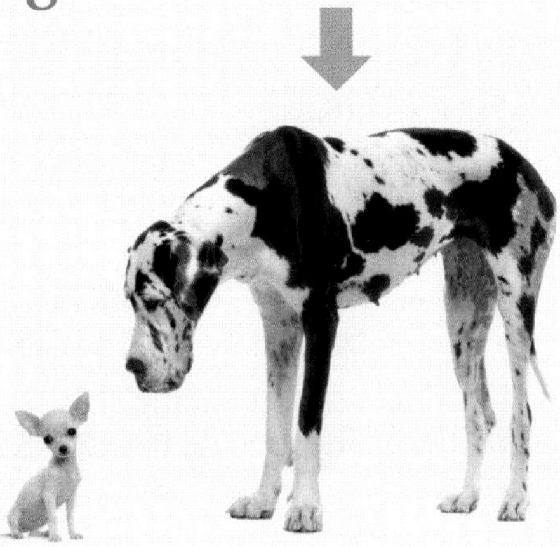

Big means not small.

bill

A **bill** is a piece of paper money.

bird

A **bird** is an animal with wings and feathers.

birthday

Your **birthday** is the day when you were born.

bite • **bit, bitten**

Bite means to cut something with your teeth.

black

Black is a color.
It is the opposite of white.

blackboard
A **blackboard** is something to write on with chalk.

blame
Blame means to say that a person did something wrong.

blanket

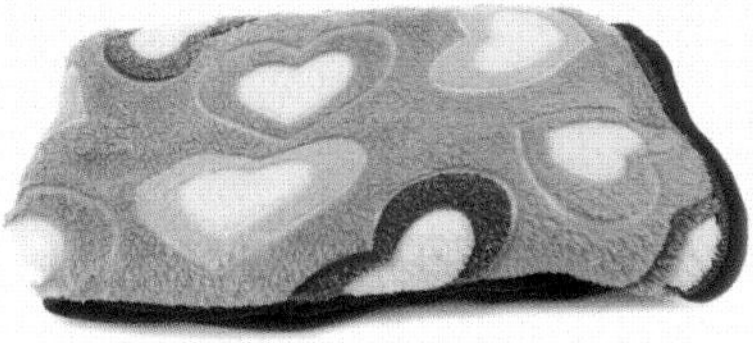

A **blanket** is a warm, thick cover for a bed.

blood
Blood is the red liquid that flows around inside your body.

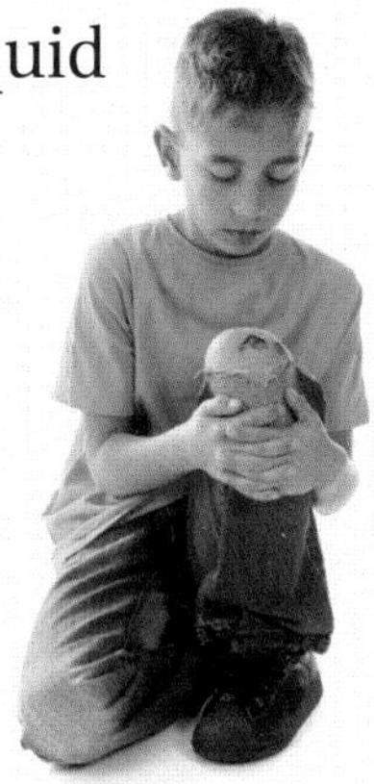

blouse
A **blouse** is a kind of shirt worn by women.

blow • blew, blown
Blow means to push out air from your mouth.

A B C D E F G H I J K L M N O P Q R S T U V W X Y Z

blue

Blue is the color of the sky when there are no clouds.

boat

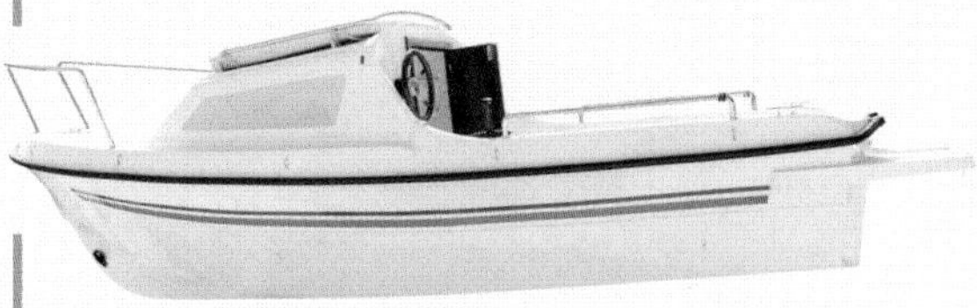

Boats use sails or a motor to carry people on water.

body • bodies

The whole of you is your **body**. People and animals have **bodies**.

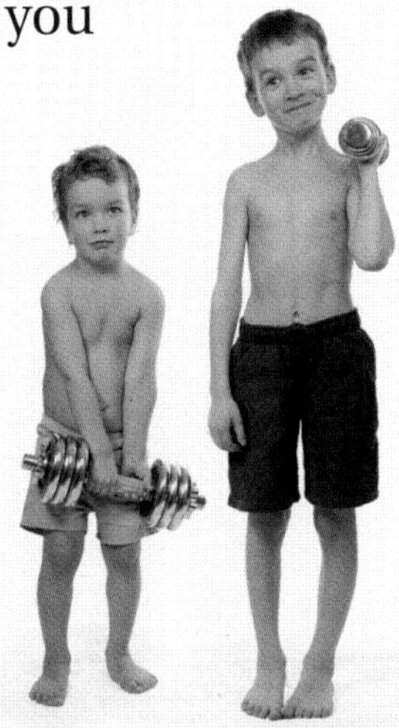

boil

Boil means to heat liquid until it bubbles.

bone

Bones are the hard parts inside a person's or animal's body.

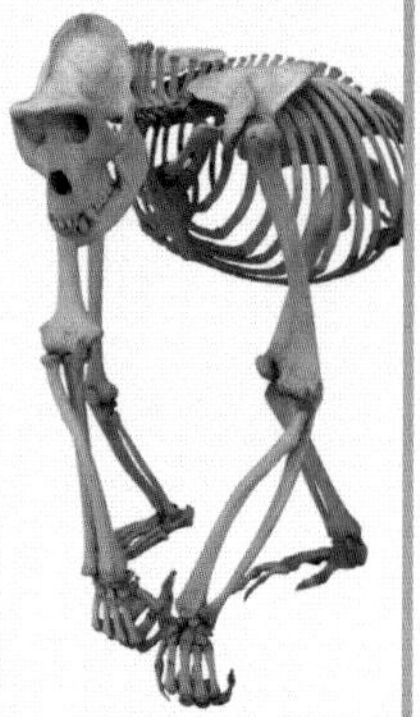

book

A **book** has pages with writing or pictures on them.

boot

Boots are shoes that cover your feet and part of your legs.

born

When a baby is **born**, it starts to live outside its mother.

borrow

If you **borrow** something, you take it and then return it.

both

Both means two people or things.

bottle

A **bottle** is something used to hold liquids.

bottom

The **bottom** is the lowest part of something.

a b c d e f g h i j k l m n o p q r s t u v w x y z

bounce

When a ball **bounces**, it moves quickly up and down.

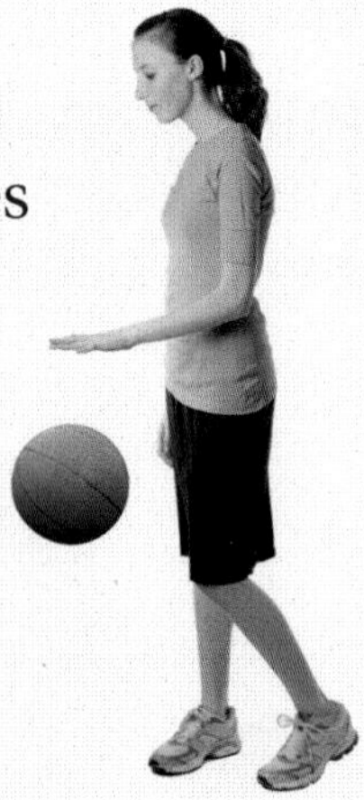

box • boxes

A **box** is made to hold things. All **boxes** have four sides and a bottom.

boy

A **boy** is a child who will grow up to be a man.

brain

The **brain** is a part of the body. It is inside the head. People think with their **brains**.

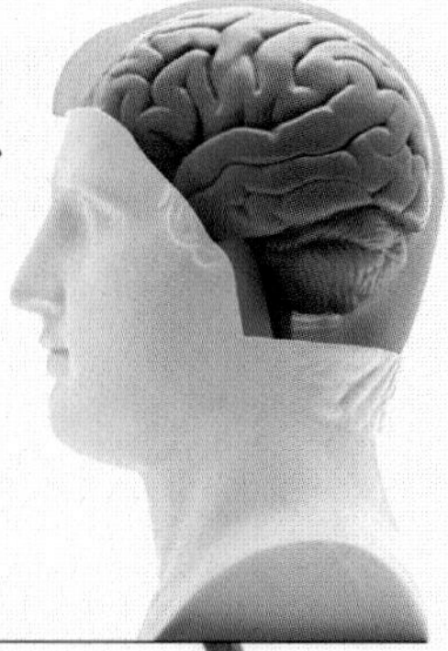

branch • branches

A **branch** is a part of a tree growing out from its trunk.

brave

Brave means not being afraid of anything.

bread

Bread is a food made with flour and baked.

break • broke, broken

Break means to make something come to pieces.

breakfast

Breakfast is the first meal of the day.

breathe

Breathe means to take air into the lungs and let it out again.

bridge

A **bridge** is used to cross over a road or river.

bright

Bright means strong in color or shining strongly.

bring • brought

Bring means to carry something to a place.

broom

A **broom** is a brush with a long handle used for sweeping.

brother

Your **brother** is a boy or man who has the same mother and father as you.

brush • brushes

A **brush** looks like a small broom. **Brushes** are used for cleaning or painting.

bubble

A **bubble** is very light and round and has air in it.

build • built

Build means to make something by putting parts together.

bulldozer
A **bulldozer** is a very large tractor. It pushes dirt and rocks from one place to another.

burn
Burn means to be on fire.

bus • buses
A **bus** is a large automobile with seats for many people.

busy

If you are **busy**, you have a lot of things to do.

butter
Butter is a food made from cow's milk. It is soft and yellow.

a
b
c
d
e
f
g
h
i
j
k
l
m
n
o
p
q
r
s
t
u
v
w
x
y
z

A
B
C
D
E
F
G
H
I
J
K
L
M
N
O
P
Q
R
S
T
U
V
W
X
Y
Z

butterfly • **butterflies**

A **butterfly** is an insect with four thin wings. These wings have bright colors.

button

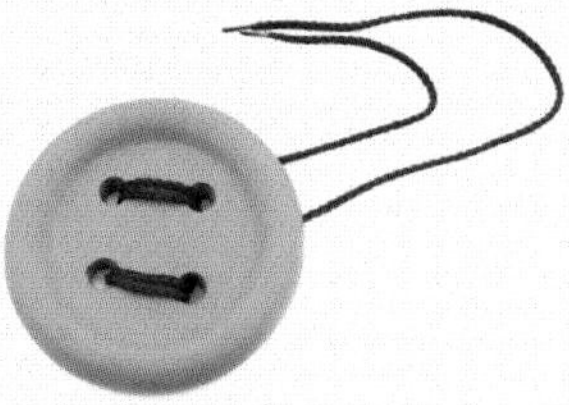

A **button** is a small, round thing on your clothes.

buy • **bought**

Buy means to pay money for something. Once you have **bought** it, it is yours.

bye

You say **bye** when you are leaving someone.

Cc Cc Cc Cc

cab

A **cab** is the same as a taxi.

cage

Animals and birds are often kept in a **cage**.

cake

A **cake** is a sweet baked food made of flour.

calendar

A **calendar** shows all the days, weeks, and months in a year.

calf • **calves**

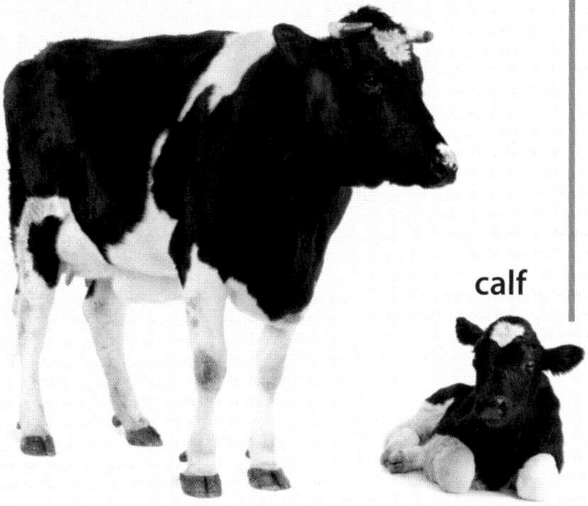

A **calf** is a baby cow.

A B C D E F G H I J K L M N O P Q R S T U V W X Y Z

call

Call means to give someone or something a name.

camel

A **camel** is an animal with a long neck and a big hump on its back.

camera

A **camera** is something used to take pictures.

camp

A **camp** is a place to live outdoors for a short time.

candle

A **candle** is a stick that makes light when you burn it.

candy • **candies**

Candy is a kind of sweet food. **Candies** may have chocolate, nuts, or fruit.

cap
A **cap** is a soft flat hat with a curved part in front.

car
A **car** is a machine with four wheels and a motor.

card
A **card** is a piece of paper with words or pictures on it.

care

Care means to look after something or someone.

careful
Careful means giving a lot of attention.

carpenter
A **carpenter** is a person whose job is to build things out of wood.

A B C D E F G H I J K L M N O P Q R S T U V W X Y Z

carrot

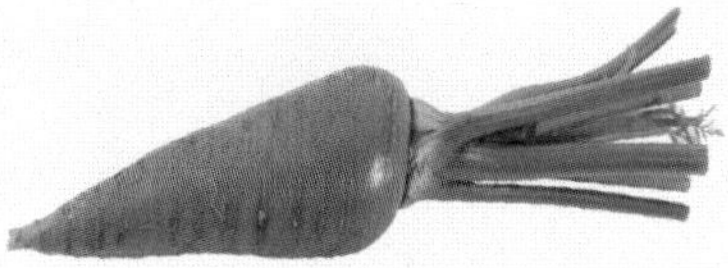

A **carrot** is a long, orange vegetable.

carry • carried

When you **carry** something, you pick it up and take it to another place.

castle

A **castle** is a large building. It is made of stone. Kings, queens, and knights lived in **castles**.

cat

A **cat** is an animal with soft fur and a long tail.

catch • caught

Catch means to get hold of something that is moving.

caterpillar

A **caterpillar** is an insect. **Caterpillars** change into butterflies or moths.

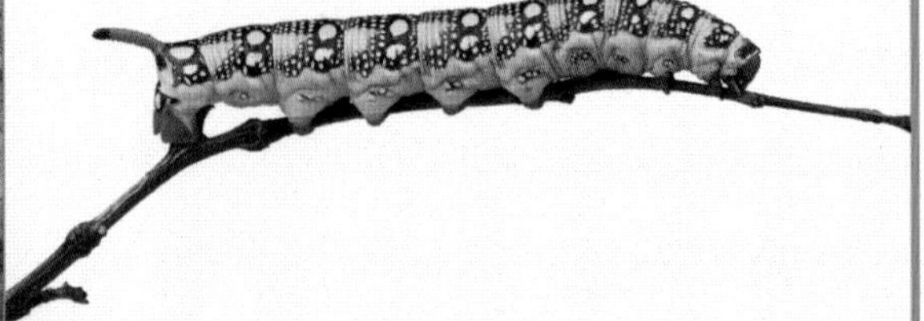

cave

A **cave** is a large hole in the side of a mountain or under the ground.

ceiling

The **ceiling** is the top part of a room. The floor is the bottom.

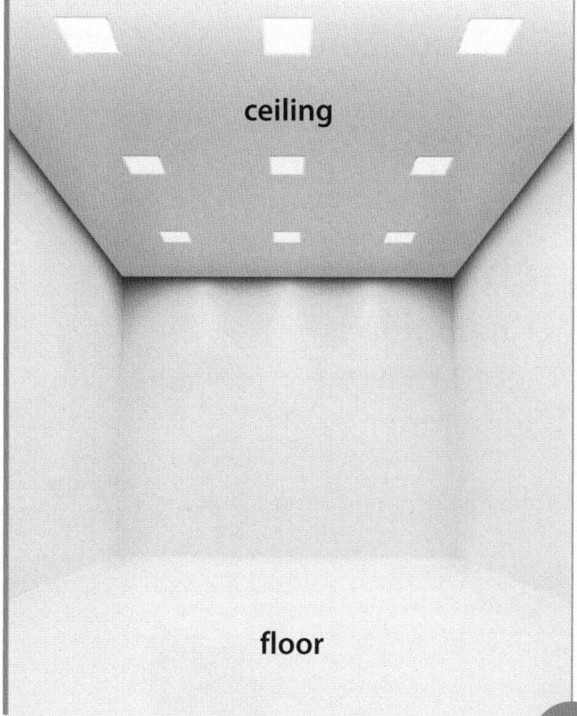

cell phone

A **cell phone** is a type of telephone that does not have wires.

center

Center is a place that is in the middle of something.

cereal

A **cereal** is a kind of food. Many **cereals** are made from corn, wheat, or rice.

a b c d e f g h i j k l m n o p q r s t u v w x y z

chain

A **chain** is made of metal rings joined together.

chair

A **chair** is a piece of furniture you sit on.

chalk

Chalk is something to write with on a blackboard.

chameleon

A **chameleon** is a type of lizard. It can change the color of its skin.

champion

Champion is another word for winner.

change

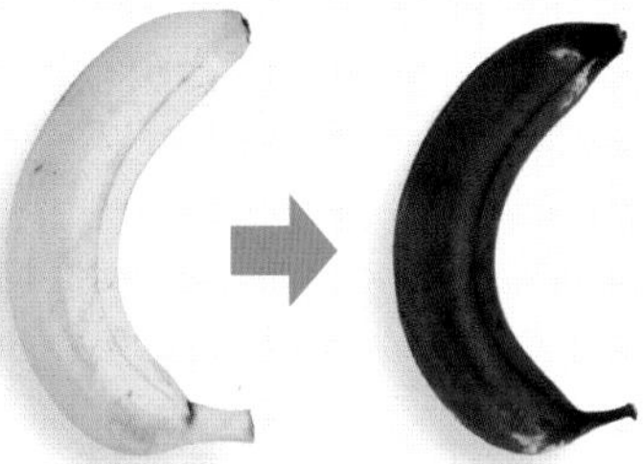

Change means to become different.

chase

Chase means to move after something.

cheap

Cheap means costing little money.

cheek

Your **cheek** is a part of the face. It is below the eye and next to the nose.

cheer

Cheer means to shout and wave your hands in the air with excitement.

cheese

Cheese is a food made from milk.

A B C D E F G H I J K L M N O P Q R S T U V W X Y Z

chest

Your **chest** is the front part of your body between your neck and your stomach.

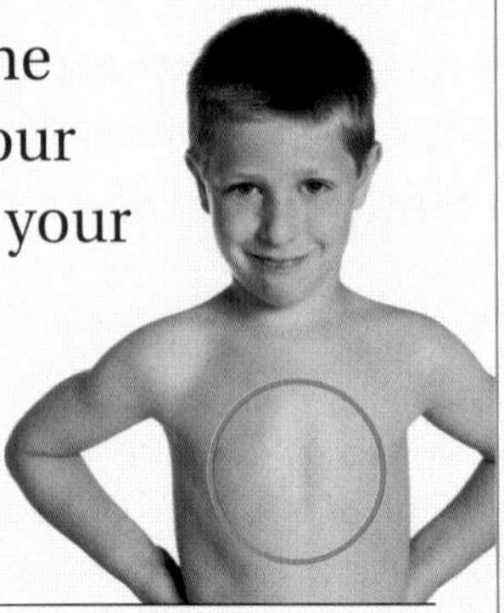

chew

Chew means to cut or bite something with the teeth.

chicken

Chickens are birds people raise for eggs and meat.

child • children

A **child** is a young boy or girl. **Children** grow up to become adults.

chimney

A **chimney** is a part of a building for carrying smoke from a fireplace.

chin

Your **chin** is the part of your face below your mouth.

chocolate

Chocolate is a brown sweet or drink made from cocoa beans.

choose • chose, chosen

Choose means to pick out something that you want to have.

Christmas

Christmas comes on December 25th, the day when people celebrate the birth of Jesus.

church • churches

A **church** is a building where Christians meet and pray.

circle

A **circle** is a round shape.

city • cities

A **city** is a very large place where many people live and work.

class • classes

A **class** is a group of students who learn together.

clean

Clean is well washed and not dirty at all.

clear

Clear means easy to see. If a sky is **clear**, it has no clouds.

climb

Climb means to move towards the top of something.

clock

A **clock** is a machine that shows you what time it is.

close

Close means to shut something.

clothes

Coats, shirts, dresses, pants, and socks are all kinds of **clothes**.

cloud

A **cloud** is made up of tiny drops of water floating together in the sky.

clown

A **clown** is a person who makes you laugh.

coat

A **coat** is clothing that you wear over your other clothes to keep you warm.

A B C D E F G H I J K L M N O P Q R S T U V W X Y Z

coffee

Coffee is a hot drink that is made by adding water to a brown powder.

color

Red, yellow, blue, and green are **colors**.

coin

A **coin** is a piece of metal used as money.

comb

Comb means to tidy your hair using a **comb**.

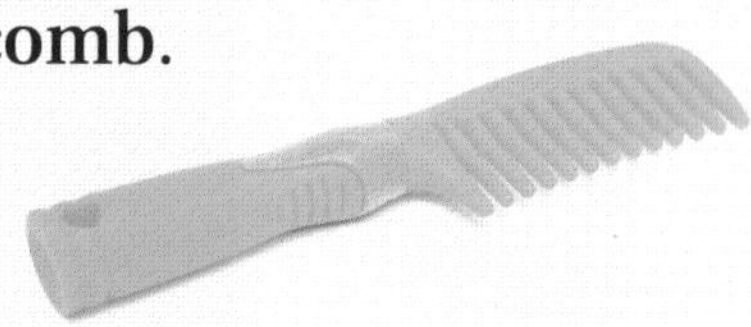

cold

Cold means not warm. When the weather is **cold**, you may feel chilly and wear a coat.

come • came, come

Come means to move near and not go away.

comfortable

Comfortable means feeling physically relaxed.

compass • compasses

You can find your way if you have a **compass**.

computer

A **computer** is a machine with a lot of uses.

contest

A **contest** is a game in which people try to win.

cook

Cook means to heat food and get it ready to eat.

cool

Cool feels a little bit warmer than cold. On a hot day, the fan feels **cool**.

A B C D E F G H I J K L M N O P Q R S T U V W X Y Z

copy • copies

Copy is a thing that is made to be the same as something else.

corn

Corn is a long, yellow vegetable that has a green covering.

corner

A **corner** is a place where two sides come together.

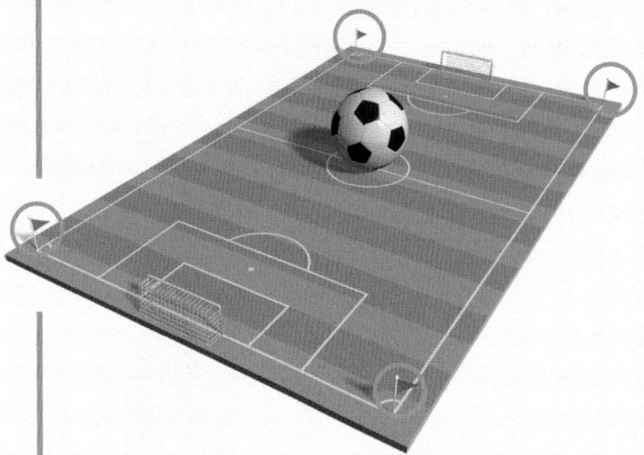

cost

Cost is the amount of money you need to buy or do something.

costume

A **costume** is clothes people wear when they pretend to be someone or something else.

cotton

Cotton is the soft white hair on the seeds of a **cotton** plant.

cough

Cough means to make a noise by making air come out of your lungs.

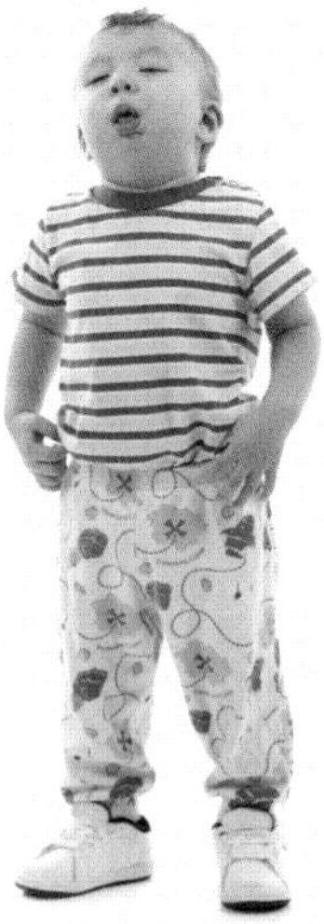

count

Count means to add up how many of something there are.

country • countries

A **country** is an area ruled by one government.

cousin

Your **cousin** is the child of your aunt or uncle.

cover

When you **cover** something, you put something else over it to hide it or keep it safe or warm.

cow

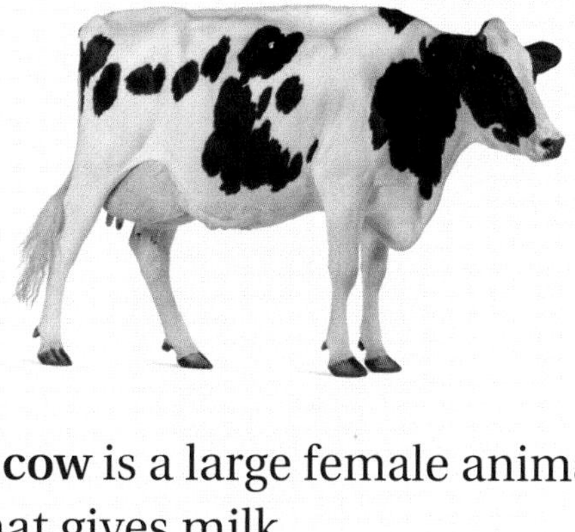

A **cow** is a large female animal that gives milk.

cowboy

A **cowboy** is a male character in a western who rides a horse.

crab

A **crab** is a sea animal with a hard shell, two claws and eight legs.

crack

A **crack** is a thin line on something where it is nearly broken.

crawl

Crawl means to go along very slowly on your hands and knees.

crayon

A **crayon** is a colored stick used for writing and drawing.

cream

Cream is the thick part on the top of milk.

crocodile

A **crocodile** is a large animal with a long body and big, sharp teeth.

crown

A **crown** is a ring of gold and jewels that kings and queens wear on their heads.

crop

Crop means vegetables, fruits, and grain that farmers grow.

cry • **cried**

Cry means to have tears come out of your eyes.

cup

A **cup** is something to drink from. It usually has a handle.

curtain

A **curtain** is a piece of cloth to cover a stage or a window.

curve

When a line turns or bends one way, it **curves**.

cushion

A **cushion** is a bag filled with soft material or feathers.

cut • **cut**

Cut means to slice something into pieces.

cute

Cute means very nice to look at.

dance

Dance means to move your body to music.

dad

Dad is a name for your father.

danger

Danger means there is something that can hurt you.

dark

Dark means no light.

a b c d e f g h i j k l m n o p q r s t u v w x y z

date

A **date** is the time shown by the day, month, or year.

daughter

A **daughter** is a person's female child.

day

A **day** lasts twenty-four hours. There are seven **days** in a week.

dead

A person, an animal, or a plant that is **dead** is not living anymore.

deaf

A person who is **deaf** cannot hear very well or cannot hear at all.

decide

Decide means to make a choice about something.

deep

If something is **deep**, it goes a long way down.

deer • deer

A **deer** is an animal with four long legs and short, brown fur.

delicious

Something good to eat tastes **delicious**.

dentist

A **dentist** is a doctor who takes care of your teeth.

A B C D E F G H I J K L M N O P Q R S T U V W X Y Z

desert

A **desert** is a place that is covered with sand.

desk

A **desk** is a table which you sit at to write or work.

dessert

Dessert is a kind of sweet food you eat at the end of a meal.

detective

A **detective** is a person who tries to solve crimes.

diamond

A **diamond** is a hard, bright, precious stone.

dictionary • dictionaries

A **dictionary** is a book that tells you the meanings of words.

die

Die means to stop living.

different

Different means not the same.

dig • dug

If you **dig**, you make a hole in the ground by moving sand or soil.

dinner

Dinner is the main meal of the day eaten in the evening.

dinosaur

Dinosaurs lived on the Earth millions of years ago. Now they are all gone.

dirty

When something is **dirty**, it is not clean.

disappear

If something **disappears**, it goes somewhere and can't be found.

disappointed

Disappointed means being sad or upset because something you hoped for did not happen.

discover

Discover means to find something.

disguise

Disguise is a thing you use to change your looks.

dish • **dishes**

A **dish** is something to put food on.

dishonest

Dishonest means not honest.

disturb

If somebody **disturbs** you, they stop you from what you are doing at the moment.

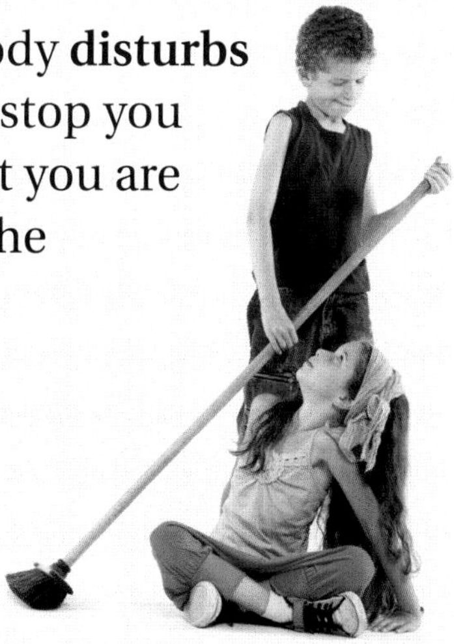

dive

Dive means to go into the water with your head first.

divide

When you **divide**, you make something whole into smaller parts.

doctor

A **doctor** is a person who takes care of sick people.

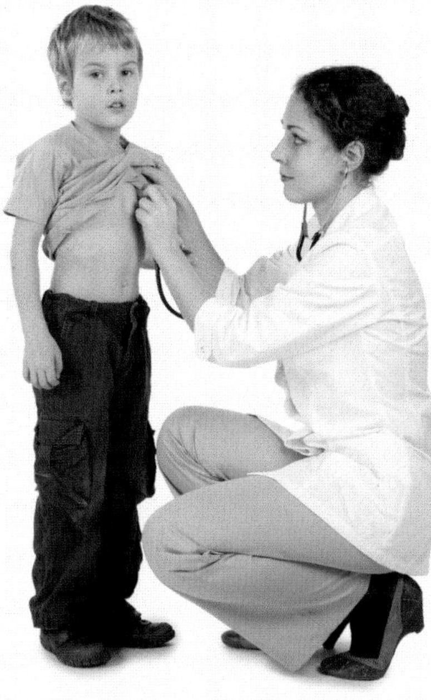

dog

A **dog** is an animal that has fur and barks. **Dogs** are usually kept as pets.

doll

A **doll** is a child's toy made to look like a person.

dolphin

A **dolphin** is a sea animal. **Dolphins** are friendly and intelligent animals.

door

To enter a room or building, you have to go in by the **door**.

dot

A **dot** is a small, round spot.

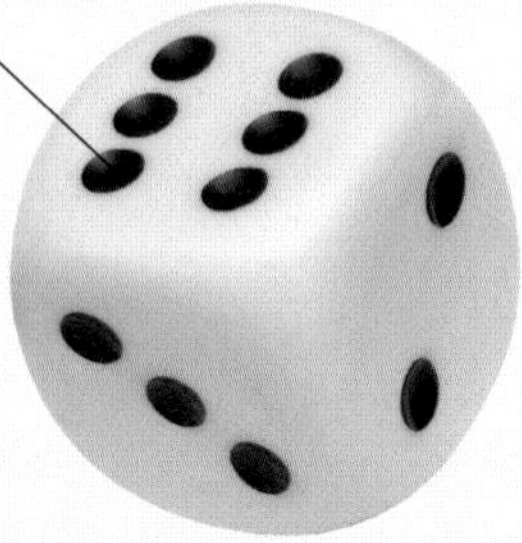

double

When something is **double**, it is twice as big or twice as many.

down

Down means going from a high place to a lower place.

dragon

Dragons are pretend creatures. They are found in fairy tales and legends.

draw • drew, drawn

Draw means to make a line to form a picture.

drawer

A **drawer** is a box that you can push in and pull out.

dream

A **dream** is a story people imagine while they sleep.

dress • dresses

A **dress** is a kind of clothing where the top and skirt is one piece.

drink • drank, drunk

Drink means to take liquid into your mouth and swallow it.

drive • drove, driven

Drive means to make something like a car or a bus move along.

drop • dropped

Drop is to let something fall.

drum

A **drum** is a musical instrument that makes a sound when you hit it.

dry

Dry means not wet.

duck

A **duck** is a water bird with short legs and a large flat beak.

dump

Dump means to drop a lot of something.

dust

Dust is a small piece of dirt.

A B C D E F G H I J K L M N O P Q R S T U V W X Y Z

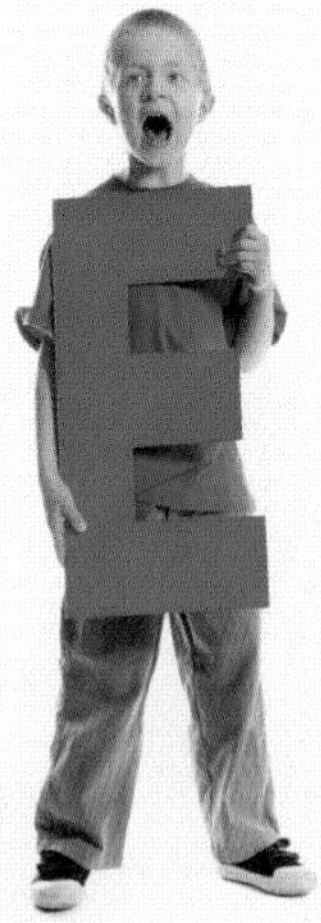

Ee *Ee* Ee *Ee*

each

Each means every thing or every person.

eagle

An **eagle** is a large bird that has very strong claws and long wings.

ear

The **ear** is a part of your body. People hear with their two **ears**.

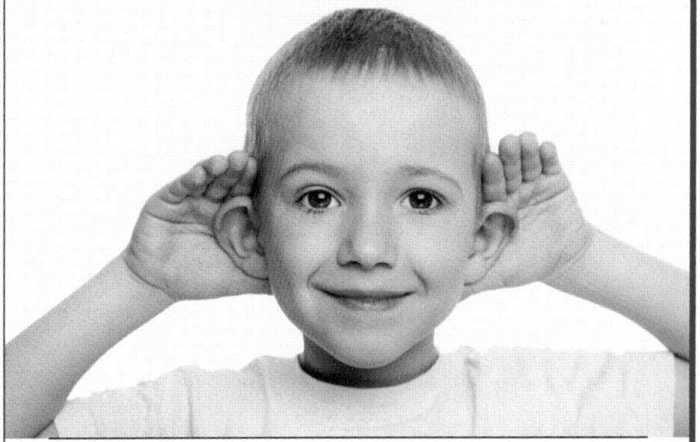

early

Early means before the usual time.

earn

Earn means to get money for doing something.

Earth

We live on a planet called **Earth**.

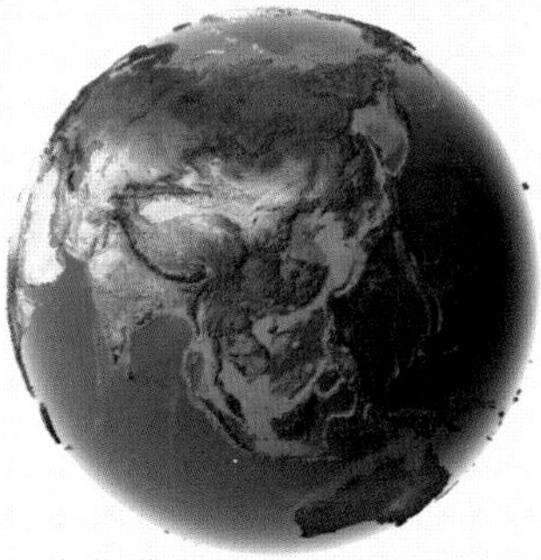

east

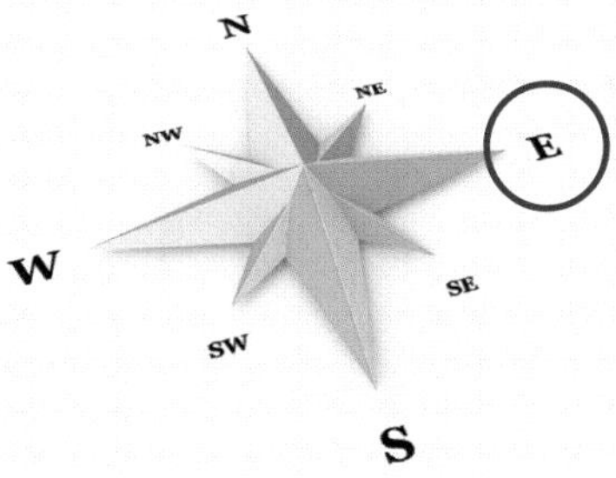

The **east** is the direction where the sun rises.

easy

Easy means not hard.

eat • ate, eaten

When you **eat,** you put food into your mouth, chew it, and swallow it.

edge

An **edge** is the end part of something.

A B C D E F G H I J K L M N O P Q R S T U V W X Y Z

egg

All birds and a few animals live inside **eggs** before they are born.

elbow

The **elbow** is the part of the body where your arm bends.

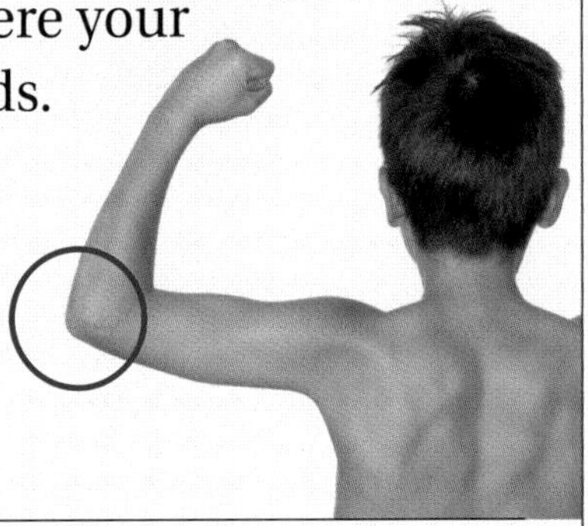

election

An **election** is a process of choosing a person for a position.

elephant

An **elephant** is a very large animal with a long nose called a trunk.

eleven

Eleven is a number between the numbers ten and twelve.

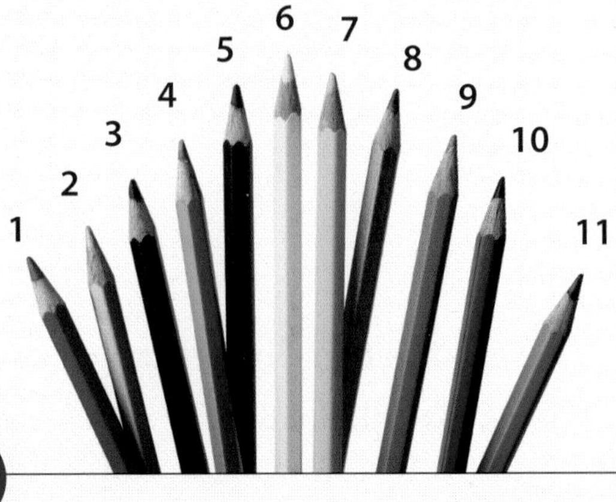

elf

An **elf** is a small magical creature with pointed ears.

end

The **end** is the final or last part of something.

email

An **email** is a message sent by computers.

enemy • **enemies**

An **enemy** is the opposite of a friend.

empty

Empty means that there is nothing inside.

engine

An **engine** produces the power to make a thing go.

a b c d e f g h i j k l m n o p q r s t u v w x y z

A B C D E F G H I J K L M N O P Q R S T U V W X Y Z

engineer

An **engineer** is someone who designs and builds engines, machines, roads, etc.

enjoy

Enjoy means to get happiness from things or experiences.

enough

Enough means as much as you need.

enter

Enter means to go into a place.

envelope

An **envelope** is a thing that covers a letter when you send it.

equal

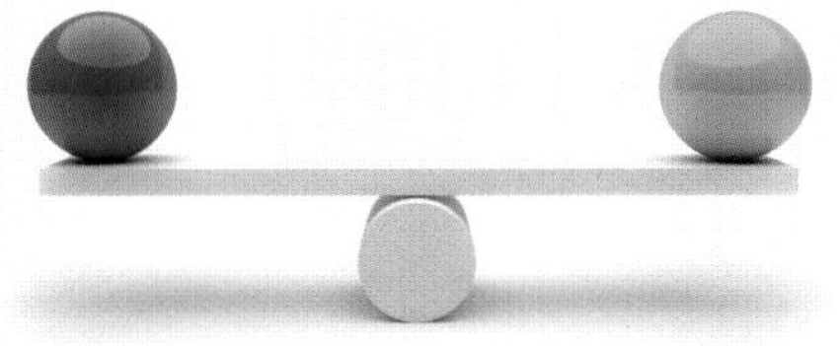

If two things are **equal**, they are the same size or number.

equator

The **equator** is an imaginary line around the middle of the Earth.

escalator

An **escalator** is a set of steps that moves up or down.

escape

Escape means to get away from something or somewhere.

evening

Evening is the time between sunset and night.

evil

Evil means very bad. The **evil** witch in a story put everybody in a castle to sleep for a hundred years.

example

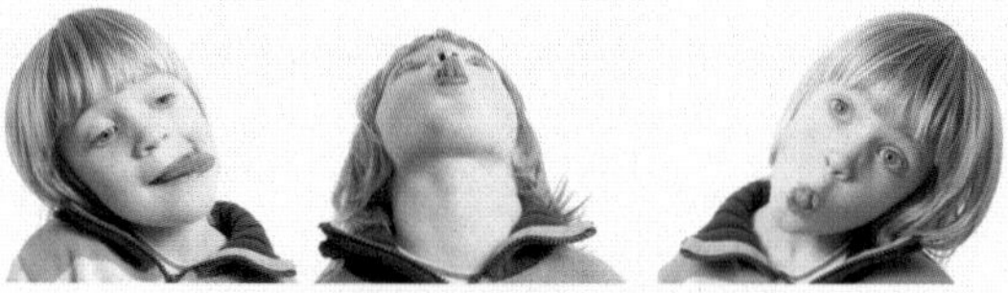

An **example** is something used to explain or describe. Sticking your tongue out at people is one **example** of bad behavior.

excellent

Excellent means very good.

excited

Excited means very happy about something.

excuse

An **excuse** is what you say to explain why you did or did not do something.

exercise

Exercise means to move your body in order to stay healthy.

exit

An **exit** is a way out of a place.

expect

If you **expect** something, you think that it will happen.

expensive

Expensive means costing a lot of money.

explain

Explain means to help someone to understand something.

explore

Explore means to go to new places and find out about them.

extra

Extra means more than is expected or usual.

eye

You have two **eyes**. They are used for seeing.

Ff Ff Ff Ff

factory • factories

A **factory** is a building where people use machines to make things.

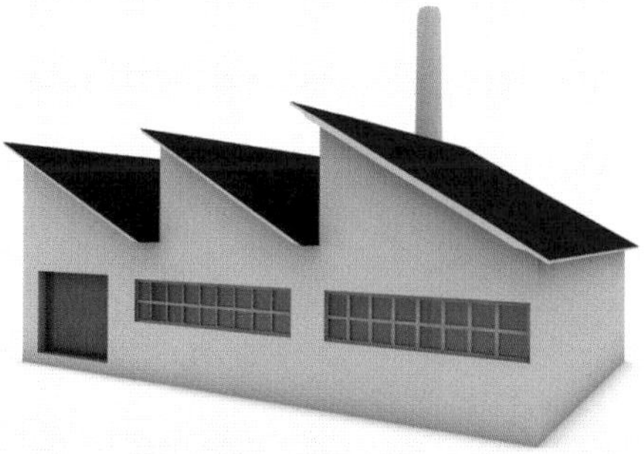

face

The **face** is the front part of your head.

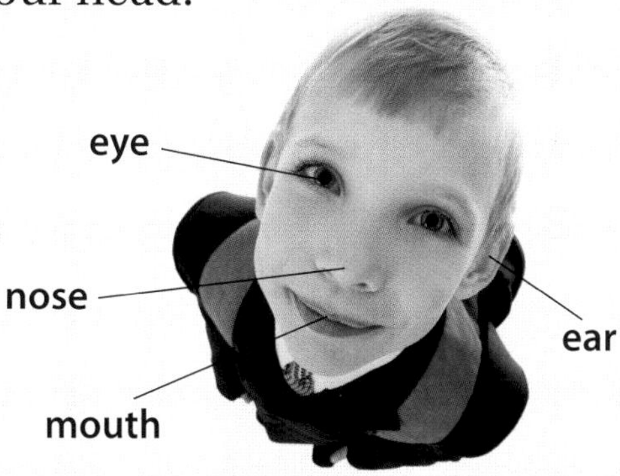

fair

Fair means equally good for everyone.

fact

A **fact** is something that is true.

fairy • fairies

A **fairy** is a small magical person in stories. Fairies often have wings.

a b c d e f g h i j k l m n o p q r s t u v w x y z

fall • fell, fallen

Fall means to come down from a high place.

false

False means not true or real.

family • families

Your **family** is your mother, your father, and your brothers and sisters.

famous

A **famous** person or thing is well known.

far
Far means away from or not close.

farm
A **farm** is a place where people grow food or keep animals.

fast
Fast means quick or moving quickly.

fat
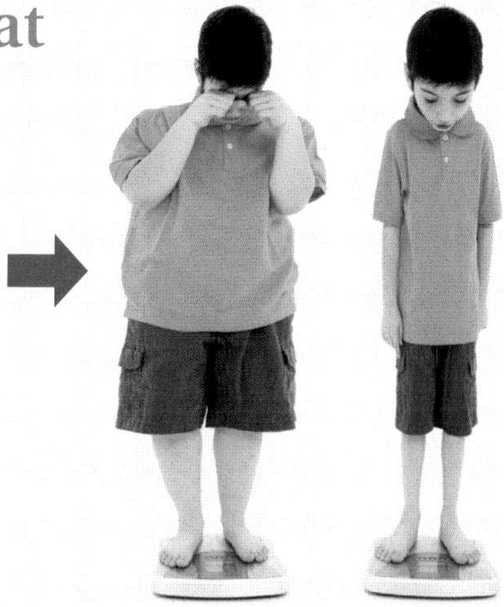

A person or animal that is **fat** has a big, round body.

father
A **father** is the male parent of his children.

A B C D E F G H I J K L M N O P Q R S T U V W X Y Z

fault

Fault means there is a mistake.

favorite

Favorite things are the things you like best.

fear

Fear means to feel you are in danger.

feather

A **feather** is something that grows on a bird's skin.

feed • fed

Feed means to give food to a person or an animal.

feel • felt

Feel means to experience a particular emotion or physical feeling.

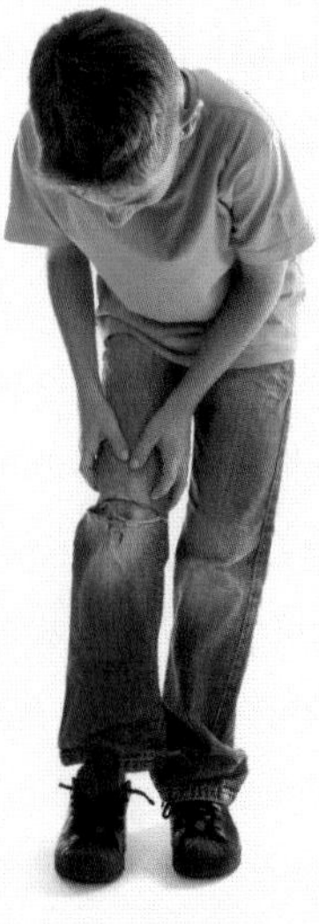

feet

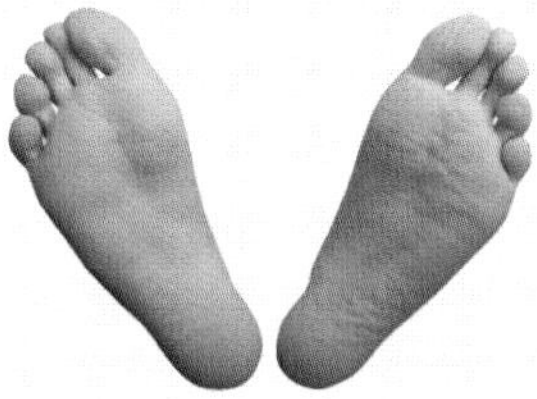

Feet means more than one **foot**.

female

A **female** person or animal belongs to the sex that can have babies.

fence

A **fence** is like a wall. It is built to make an area of land.

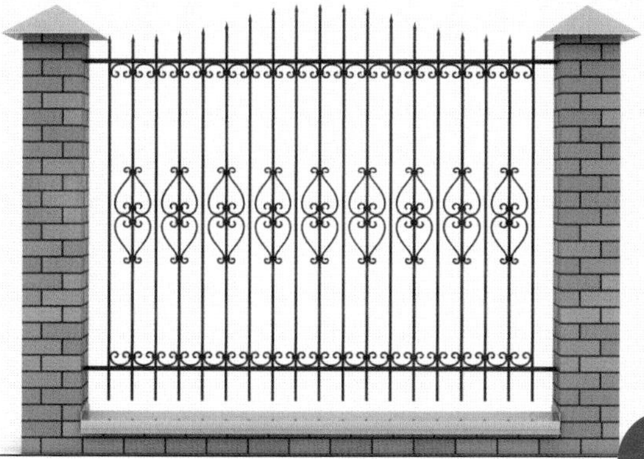

fever

When you have a **fever**, your body is hotter than usual.

few

A **few** means only a small number of people or things.

field

A **field** is an area of land covered with grass.

fierce

Fierce means angry and behaving in a violent way.

fight • fought

When two things or people **fight**, they hit or kick each other.

fill

Fill means to leave no space for any more.

find • found

When you **find** something, you see what you were looking for.

fine

Fine means very good.

finger

A **finger** is a part of your hand. People have five **fingers** on each hand.

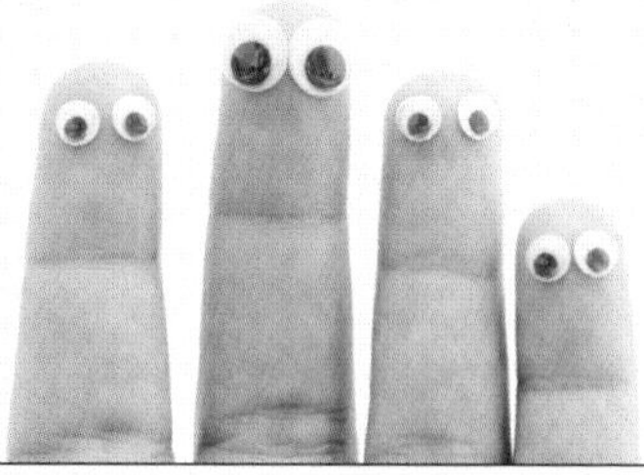

finish

Finish means to come to the end of something.

fire

If something is on **fire**, it is burning.

fire engine

A **fire engine** is a truck that carries the things needed to put out a fire.

firefighter

A **firefighter** is a person who puts out fires.

first

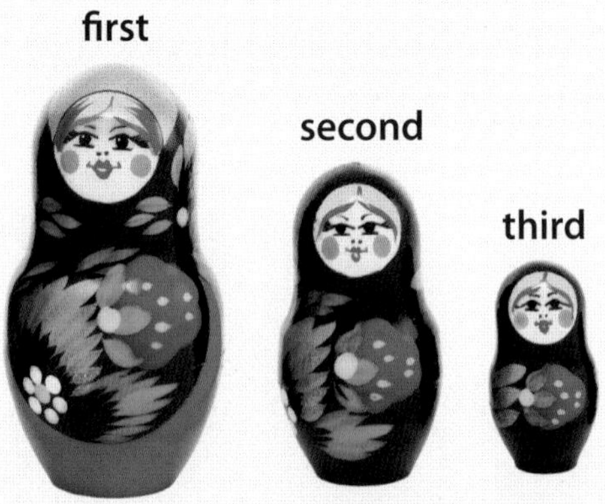

First means something that comes before everything else.

fish • fish

A **fish** is a swimming animal which lives in the water.

fist

A **fist** is a hand that is tightly closed.

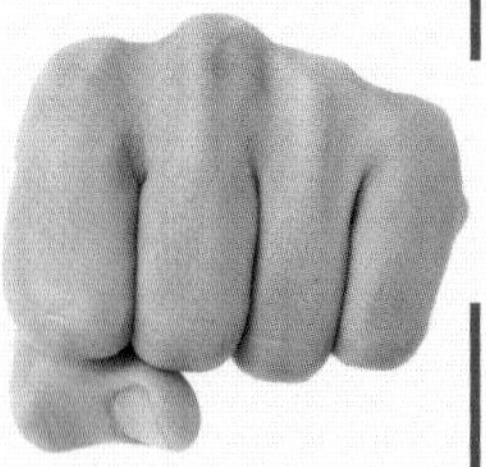

fit • fitted

Fit means to be the right size.

fix

If you **fix** something that is broken, you make it useful again.

flag

A **flag** is a piece of cloth with a symbol on it. Each country has a **flag** of its own.

flame

A **flame** is part of a fire. It is very hot.

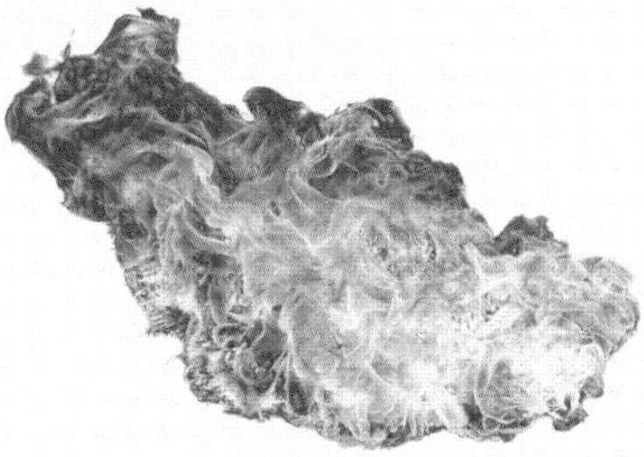

flashlight

A **flashlight** is a kind of lamp. People carry **flashlights** at night.

flat

Flat means smooth and having no parts that are higher than the rest.

float

Float means to move along slowly on water or in the air.

floor

A **floor** is the part of a room that you walk on.

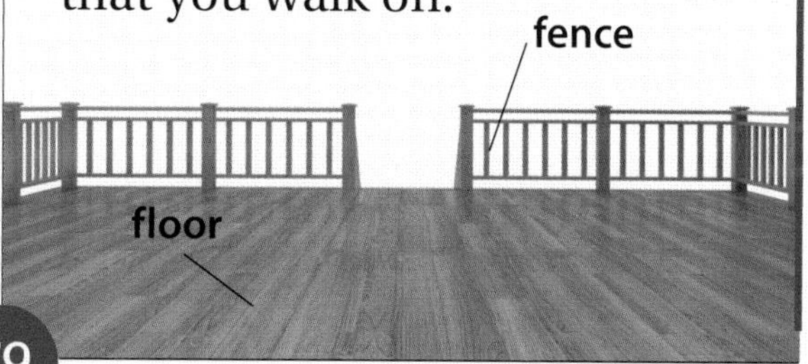

flour

Flour is the soft, white powder made from grain and used to make bread and cakes.

flower

A **flower** is the pretty part of a plant.

flu

The **flu** is something that makes you sick.

fly • **flew, flown**

Fly means to move through the air.

fold

Fold means to bend one part of a thing over another part.

follow

Follow means to come or go after someone or something.

food

Food is something that people or animals eat. It helps keep them alive.

foot • **feet**

The **foot** is at the end of the leg. The toes and the heel are part of the **foot**.

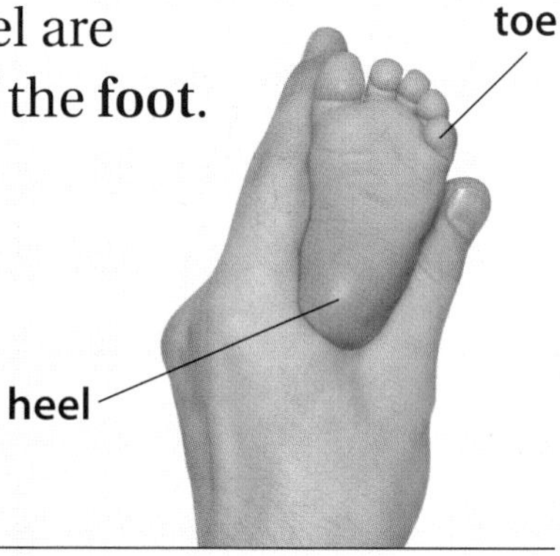

football

Football is a game played on a large field by two teams using an oval ball.

footprint

A **footprint** is a mark made by a foot or shoe.

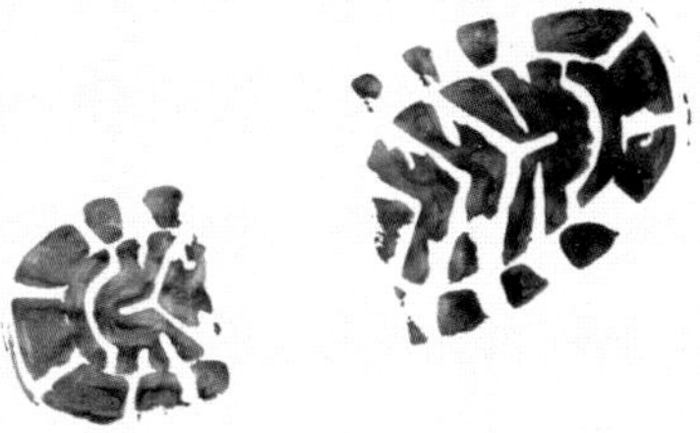

forest

A **forest** is a large area with many trees and other plants.

forget • forgot, forgotten

Forget means to not remember something.

fork

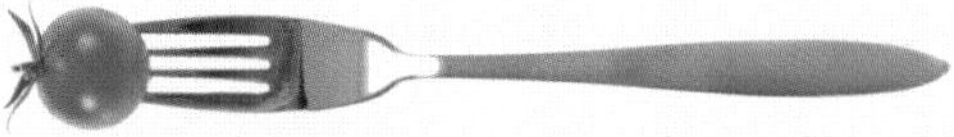

A **fork** is something that you eat food with.

forward

Forward means ahead.

fossil

A **fossil** is a dead animal or plant that has turned to stone after it has been in the ground for a long time.

fountain

A **fountain** is a jet of water that shoots up into the air.

fox • foxes

A **fox** is a wild animal with red-brown fur and a long, thick tail.

frame

A **frame** is the wooden or metal part around something like a picture.

freeze • froze, frozen

When water **freezes**, it gets very cold and turns to ice.

fresh

Fresh means picked or produced recently.

friend

A **friend** is someone you like very much.

friendly

Friendly means acting like a friend.

A B C D E F G H I J K L M N O P Q R S T U V W X Y Z

frighten

Frighten means to make someone afraid.

frog

A **frog** is a small animal. It has smooth skin and long, strong back legs. **Frogs** live near water.

front

The **front** is the part that faces forward.

frost

Frost is very thin ice. It forms when the temperature drops below 0˚C.

frown

Frown means to push your eyebrows down.

fruit

The **fruit** is a part of a plant. It has the seeds of the plant in it.

fry • fried

When you **fry** food, you cook it in hot fat or oil.

full

Full means holding as much or many as something can.

fun

Fun means doing something that makes you feel good.

fur

Fur is the hair that covers an animal's body.

furniture

Chairs, tables, beds, and desks are all kinds of **furniture**. People work on, eat on, and sleep on **furniture**.

game
A **game** is a way to play or have fun. Every **game** has rules.

garage
A **garage** is a building where cars are kept.

garden
A **garden** is a space, usually around a house, for growing flowers and vegetables.

gate
A **gate** is something that opens or shuts the way to a place.

gather

Gather means to bring things or people together to one place.

gentleman

A **gentleman** is a man who is polite and always behaves well.

ghost

A **ghost** means the spirit of a dead person.

giant

A **giant** is someone who is very big and strong.

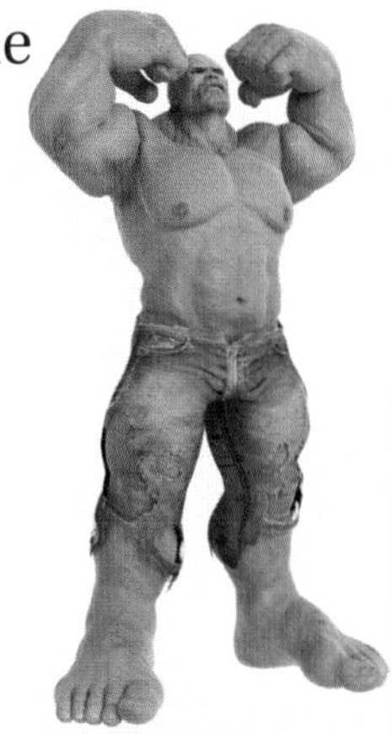

gift

A **gift** is something that you give someone as a present.

giraffe

A **giraffe** is a very tall animal with long, thin legs and a very long neck.

A B C D E F G H I J K L M N O P Q R S T U V W X Y Z

girl

A **girl** is a child who will grow up to be a woman.

give • **gave, given**

Give means to let someone have something to keep.

glass • **glasses**

Glass is a clear hard material used for windows and bottles.

glove

A **glove** is a covering for the hand with separate parts for each finger.

go • **went, gone**

Go means to move to another place.

goat

A **goat** is an animal that is kept for milk and its hairy coat.

gold

Gold is a shiny, yellow metal that people use to make jewelry, coins, and other things.

good

Good means fine. If something is **good**, people like it.

goodbye

Goodbye is the last word that one person says to another when they talk.

goose • geese

A **goose** is a big water bird with a long neck.

government

The **government** is what rules a country.

grandparent

The **grandparent** is the parent of someone's mother or father.

grass • grasses

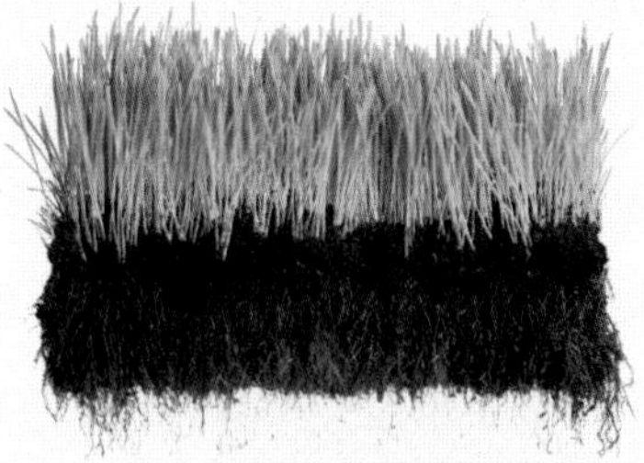

Grass is a plant with thin, green leaves that covers fields.

grasshopper

A **grasshopper** is an insect with strong back legs for jumping.

great

Great means very important and famous.

grocery store

A **grocery store** is a place that sells food and other things.

ground

Ground is the rocks and dirt on the earth.

group

People or things that are together are a **group**.

grow • grew, grown

Grow means to get bigger.

growl

Growl means to make a loud, deep sound.

A B C D E F G H I J K L M N O P Q R S T U V W X Y Z

guard

A **guard** is a person who watches over something.

guess

Guess means to try to think of an answer to something you don't know.

guest

A **guest** is a person who comes to visit you.

gun

A **gun** is a dangerous weapon that fires bullets.

gym

A **gym** is a room where people play games and do exercises.

habit

A **habit** is something that you do very often, without thinking about it.

hair

Hair is what grows on the head.

hairdresser

A **hairdresser** is a person who cuts, washes, and shapes hair.

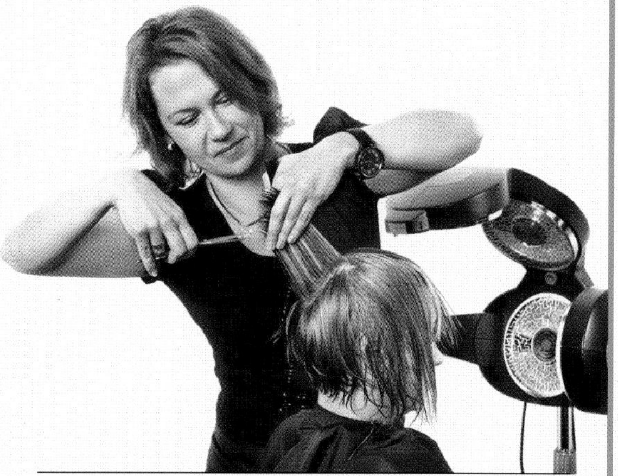

half • halves

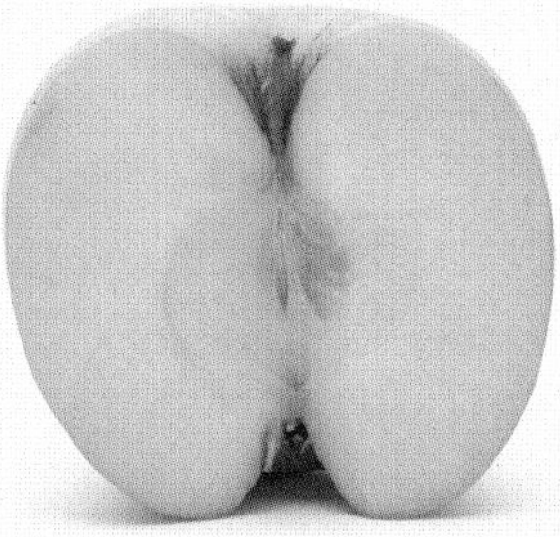

A **half** is one of two equal parts of something.

A
B
C
D
E
F
G
H
I
J
K
L
M
N
O
P
Q
R
S
T
U
V
W
X
Y
Z

Halloween

Halloween is a holiday on the last day of October. Children dress up in costumes on **Halloween**.

ham

Ham is meat from the top of the back leg of a pig.

hamburger

A **hamburger** is a round sandwich with meat in it.

hammer

A **hammer** is a tool used for hitting nails into wood or walls.

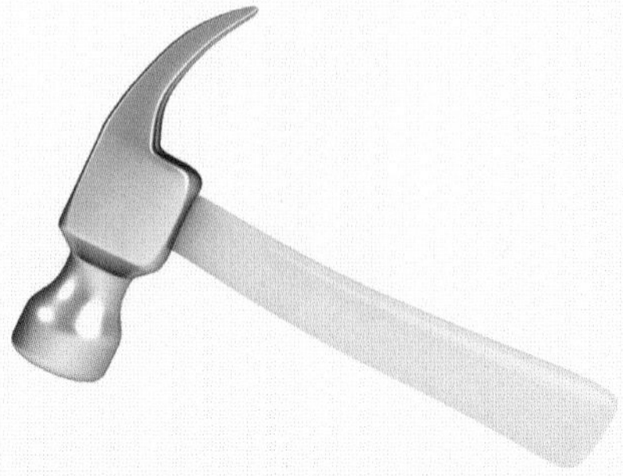

hamster

A **hamster** is a small animal with short fur and a short tail.

hand

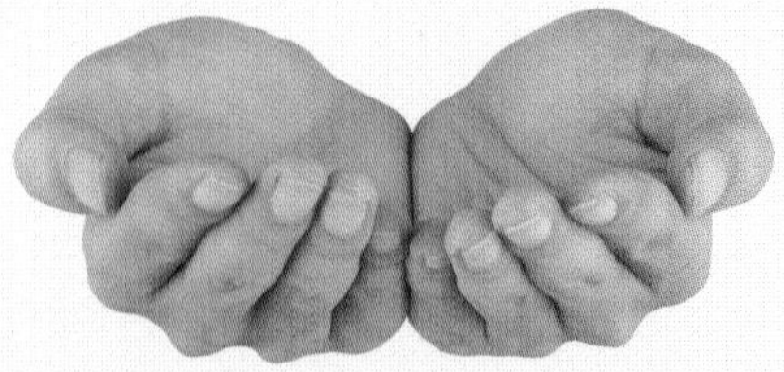

A **hand** is the part of your body at the end of your arm.

handle

A **handle** is the part of something that you hold in your hand.

handsome

Handsome means good-looking.

hang • **hung**

Something that is **hanging** is joined at the top to something above it.

hanger

A **hanger** is something to hang clothes on.

happy

Happy means to feel very good about something.

hard

Hard means solid and firm.

harm

Harm is physical injury to a person or an animal.

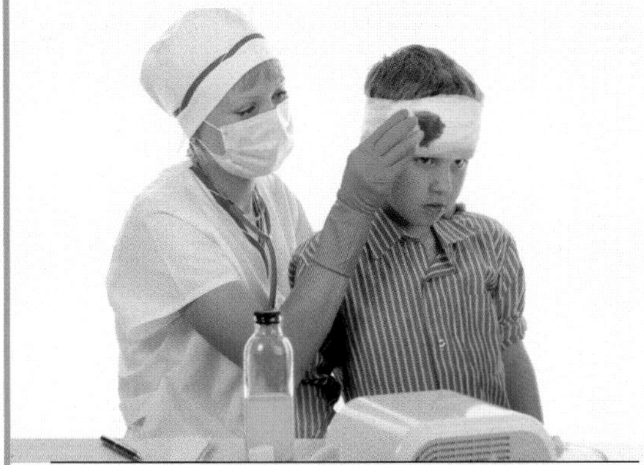

harvest

Harvest means to gather all the crops when they are ready.

hat

A **hat** is something to wear on your head.

hatch

When a baby chicken breaks out of its egg, it **hatches**.

hate

Hate means to not like something very much.

head

Your **head** is the top part of your body.

hear • heard

Hear means to get sounds through your ears.

heart

The **heart** is a part of the body. It makes the blood move through the body.

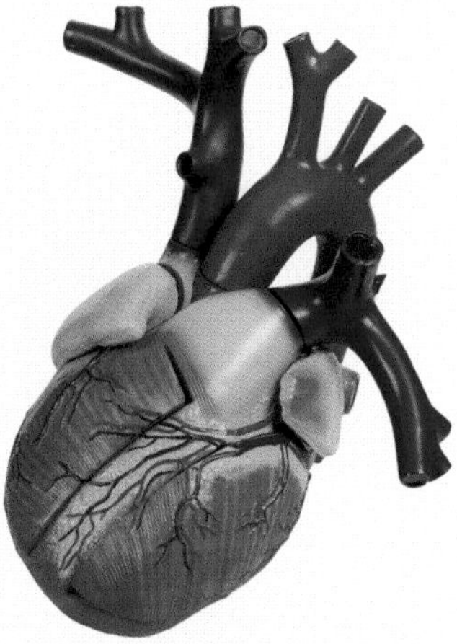

heat

Heat means a form of energy or the state of being hot.

heavy

Heavy means hard to lift or carry.

A
B
C
D
E
F
G
H
I
J
K
L
M
N
O
P
Q
R
S
T
U
V
W
X
Y
Z

heel

The back of your foot or the back of your shoe is a **heel**.

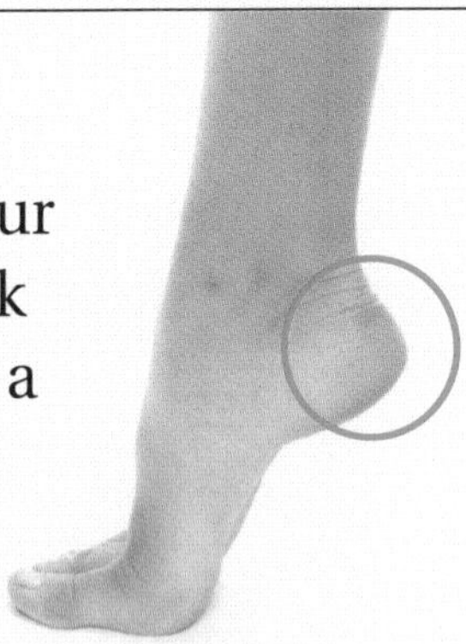

height

Your **height** is the distance from the ground to the top of your head.

helicopter

A **helicopter** is a flying vehicle. It is lifted by its long blades on top.

hello

Hello is a word people say when they meet.

helmet

A **helmet** is a hard hat which protects the head.

help

Help means to make things easier for another person.

hen

A **hen** is a female chicken.

hide • hid, hidden

When you **hide**, you go to a place where people cannot see you.

high

High means tall or far from the ground.

hill

A **hill** is a small mountain with gently sloping sides.

hit • hit

Hit means to touch hard against something.

hold • held

Hold means to have something in your hands or arms.

a b c d e f g h i j k l m n o p q r s t u v w x y z

hole

A **hole** is an open space in something.

home

Home is the place where you live.

homework

Homework is school work that you do at home.

honest

To be **honest** is to be truthful.

honey

Honey is a sweet, sticky liquid made by bees.

hop • hopped

Hop means to jump on one foot.

hope

If you **hope** for something, you really want it to happen.

horn

A **horn** is a hard, often curved part on the heads of some animals.

horse

A **horse** is a large, four-legged animal often used for riding and pulling.

hospital

A **hospital** is a place where sick people go to get better.

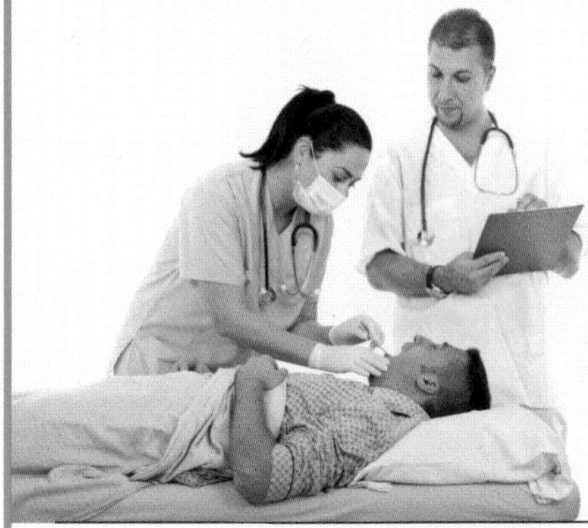

hot

Hot is the opposite of cold. It means very warm.

hot dog

A **hot dog** is a cooked sausage in a long piece of bread.

hotel

A **hotel** is a building where people pay to stay in a room.

hour

An **hour** is an amount of time equal to 60 minutes.

house

A **house** is a place where people live.

housewife • housewives

A **housewife** is a woman who looks after her home and children.

hug • hugged

Hug means to put your arms around someone or something.

huge

Huge means very big.

human

Human means of or like a person.

hungry

Hungry means wanting something to eat.

hurt • **hurt**

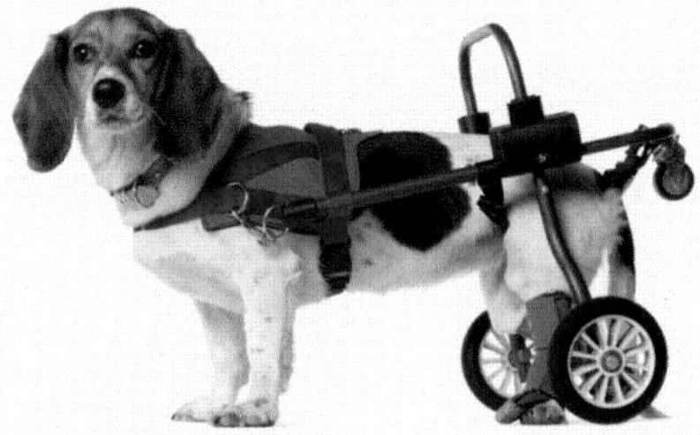

Hurt means to cause pain or feel pain.

hurry • **hurried**

Hurry means to move quickly.

husband

A **husband** is the man that a woman is married to.

Ii *Ii* Ii *Ii*

ice cream

Ice cream is a frozen food made from milk, cream, and sugar.

idea

An **idea** is something that you think of.

I

I means the person who is speaking or writing.

ice

Ice is frozen water. It is cold and hard.

ill

Ill means sick or not feeling well.

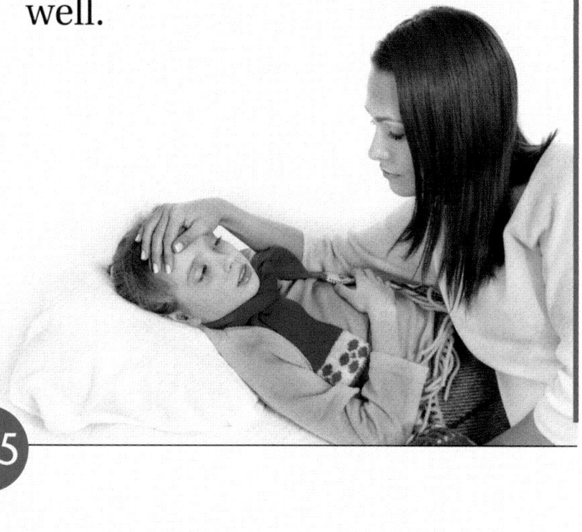

in
In means inside.

inch • **inches**

An **inch** is a unit of length equal to 2.54cm.

ink
Ink is the colored liquid that is used for writing or printing.

insect

An **insect** is a very small animal with six legs.

inside
Inside means the inner side of something.

instrument
Music is played on an **instrument**. Pianos, trumpets, drums, violins, and guitars are all **instruments**.

inventor

An **inventor** thinks of something useful that no one has ever thought of before.

iron

An **iron** is a tool that we use to make clothes smooth.

island

An **island** is a piece of land surrounded by water.

A B C D E F G H I J K L M N O P Q R S T U V W X Y Z

MFE-D-j

Jj *Jj* Jj *Jj*

jar

A **jar** is a container with a wide opening at the top.

jacket

A **jacket** is a short coat with sleeves.

jam

Jam is made by boiling sugar and fruit together.

jeans

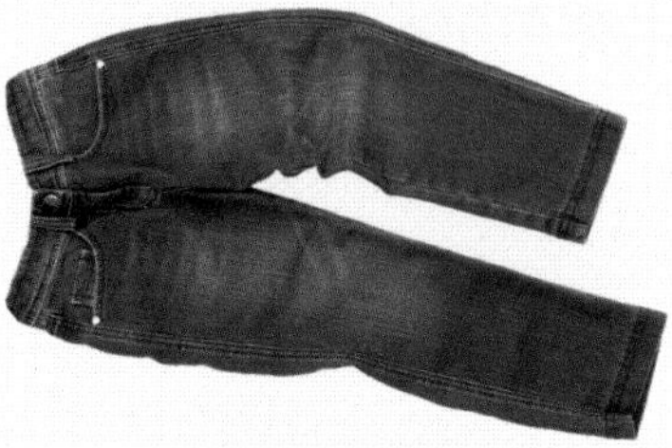

Jeans are pants that are made of thick cotton cloth called denim.

jewel

A **jewel** is a precious stone.

job

A **job** is the work that someone does to earn money.

jog • **jogged**

Jog means to run slowly, often for exercise.

juggle

Juggle means to balance objects and keep them in the air.

juice

Juice is the liquid from fruit and vegetables.

jump

When you **jump**, you use your legs to go into the air.

just

Just means only a short time ago.

Kk *Kk* Kk *Kk*

kangaroo

A **kangaroo** is an animal with strong back legs for jumping.

ketchup

Ketchup is a very thick, red liquid. It is made from tomatoes.

kettle

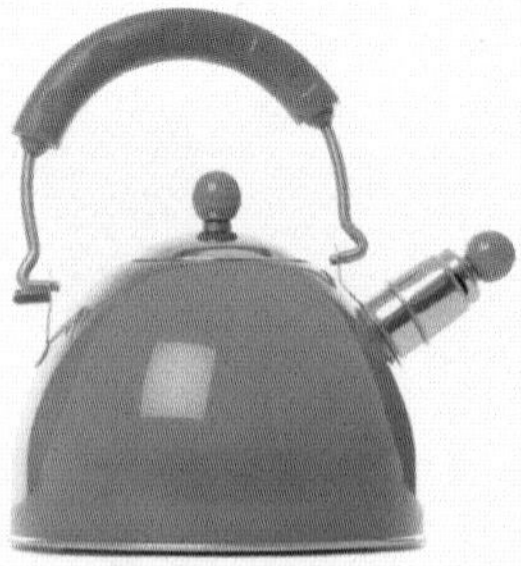

A **kettle** is a kind of pot. You boil water in a **kettle**.

key

A **key** is a piece of metal that opens a lock.

kick

Kick means to hit something with your foot.

kid

A **kid** is a word for a child.

kill

Kill means to make a living thing die.

kind

A **kind** person is nice to other people and ready to help them.

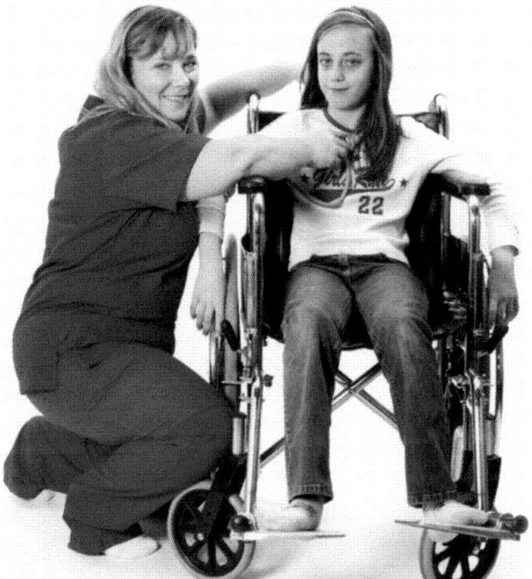

king

A **king** is a man who rules a country.

kingdom

A **kingdom** is a country a king or queen rules over.

kiss

Kiss means to touch someone with your lips.

kitchen

A **kitchen** is a room where food is cooked.

kite

A **kite** is a toy you can fly with strings.

kitten

A **kitten** is a baby cat.

knee

A **knee** is the part of the body in the center of the leg that bends.

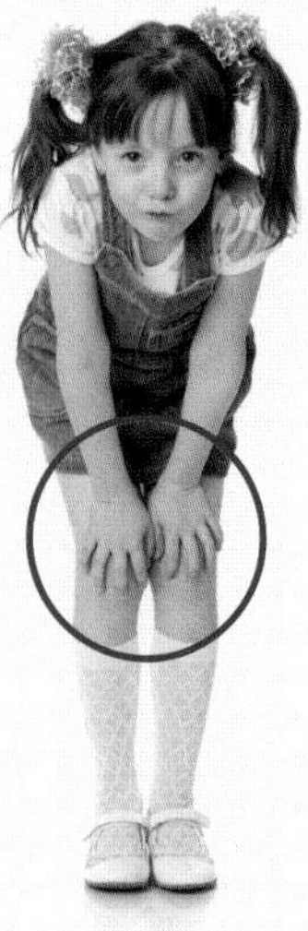

knife • knives

A **knife** is a tool for cutting. It is a sharp piece of metal.

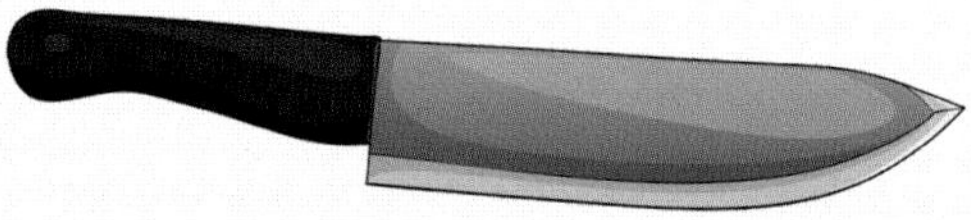

koala

A **koala** is an animal that looks like a small bear. It lives in trees.

Ll *Ll* Ll *Ll*

lake

A **lake** is an area of water with land all around it.

ladder

A **ladder** is used to climb up and down.

lamb

A **lamb** is a baby sheep.

ladybug

A **ladybug** is a small, round beetle that can fly.

lamp

A **lamp** is used to make light.

A B C D E F G H I J K L M N O P Q R S T U V W X Y Z

land

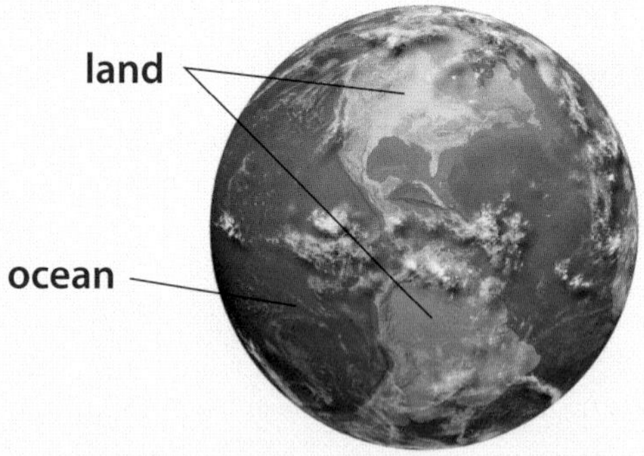

Land is the part of the world that is not water.

language

Language is the way people understand each other when they talk or write.

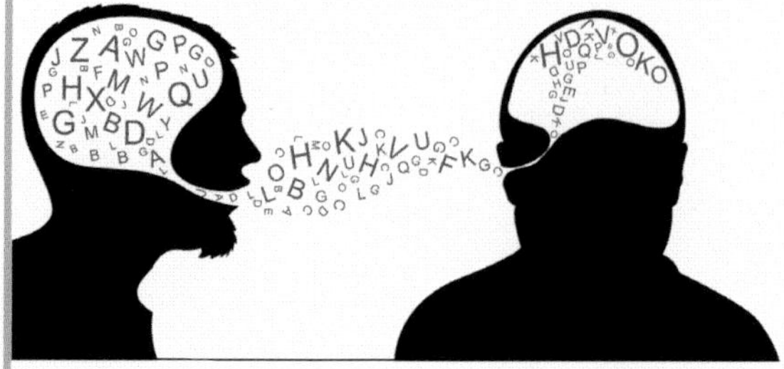

lantern

A **lantern** is a lamp with glass sides and a handle on top.

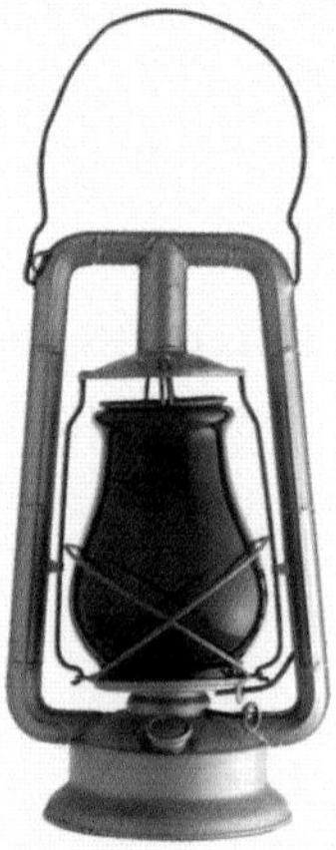

lap

The **lap** is the top part of the legs of a person who is sitting.

large

Large means big.

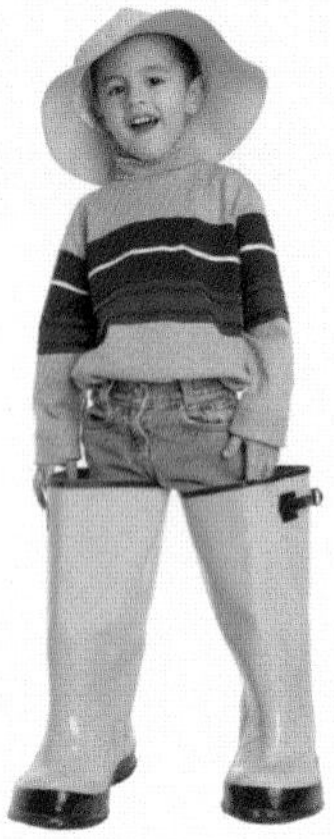

laugh

When people see something funny, they **laugh**.
Ha! Ha!

launch

When you **launch** a rocket into space, you start it moving.

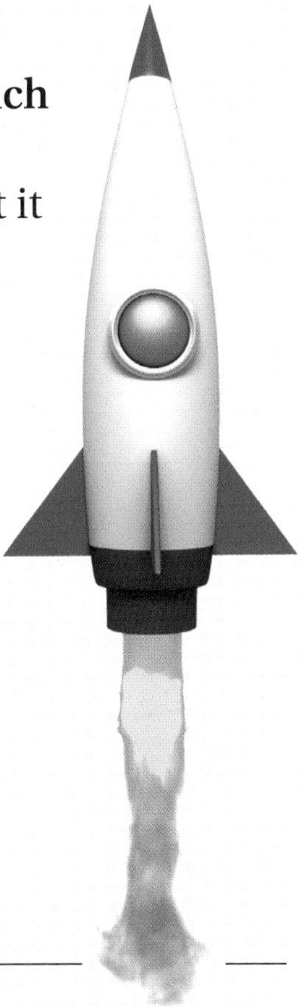

laundry • laundries

Laundry is dirty clothes that are ready to be washed.

law

A **law** is a rule that people agree to share.

lawn

A **lawn** is a place where grass grows.

lawyer

A **lawyer** is a person who is trained to advise people about law.

lazy

A **lazy** person does not want to do any work.

lead • led

Lead means to show the way.

leaf • leaves

A **leaf** is one of the green parts of a plant or tree.

leak

Leak means to escape through a small hole.

learn

You **learn** if you find out facts or get to know how to do things.

leave • left

Leave means to go away.

left

Left is the opposite of the right side.

leg

The **leg** is a part of the body. People and animals walk on their **legs**.

lemon

A **lemon** is a yellow fruit with a thick skin and a sour taste.

lesson

A **lesson** is something to be learned or studied.

A B C D E F G H I J K L M N O P Q R S T U V W X Y Z

letter
A **letter** is a message that you write on paper to another person.

lettuce

Lettuce is a plant with large green leaves, often eaten in salad.

library • libraries
A **library** is a place where books are kept.

lick

Lick means to touch something using the tongue.

lid
A **lid** is a cover over a box or other container.

lift
Lift means to pick something up.

light

Light comes from the sun. At night, lamps give us **light**.

lighthouse

Lighthouses are built near shores. Their lights keep ships from danger.

like

Like means to be fond of something.

line

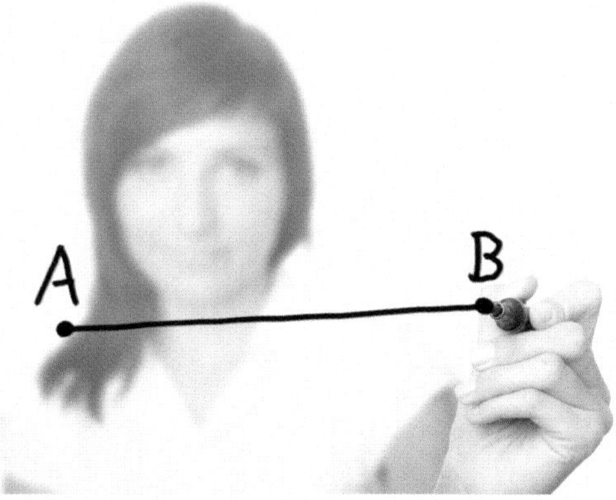

A **line** is a long thin mark. **Lines** can be curved or straight.

lion

A **lion** is a large dangerous wild cat. A female **lion** is called a lioness.

a b c d e f g h i j k l m n o p q r s t u v w x y z

A B C D E F G H I J K L M N O P Q R S T U V W X Y Z

lip

A **lip** is one of the edges of the mouth.

liquid

You can pour a **liquid**. It flows and is always wet. Water, milk, and juice are **liquids**.

list

A **list** is a group of words or names that are written down one after the other.

listen

Listen means to try to hear sounds carefully.

little

Little means small in size or not much.

live

Live means to have your home in a place.

lock

A **lock** is something that keeps a door or a gate closed.

log

A **log** is a piece of wood. **Logs** are cut from trees.

long

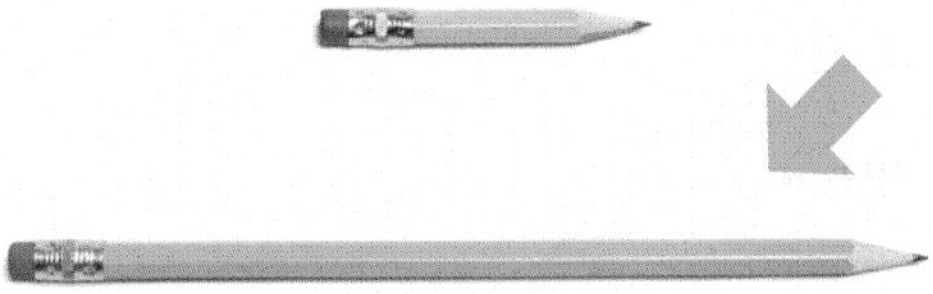

Long means great in length and distance.

look

Look means to move your eyes to see or find something.

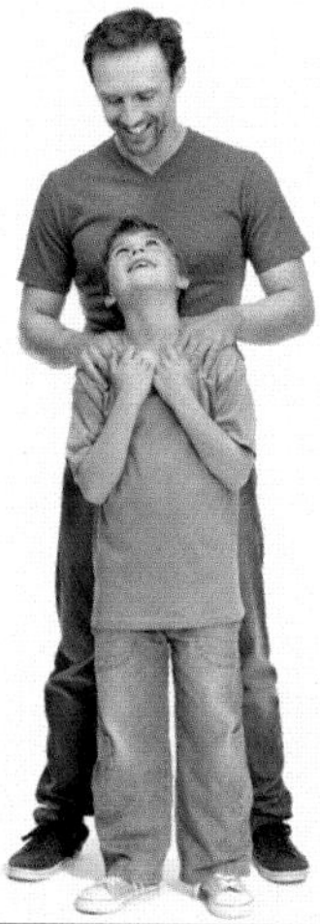

loose

Loose means not tight.

A B C D E F G H I J K L M N O P Q R S T U V W X Y Z

loud

Loud means making a lot of noise.

love

Love means to like someone or something as much as you possibly can.

low

Low means not high or tall.

lunch

Lunch is a meal eaten between breakfast and dinner.

MFE-D-m

Mm *Mm* Mm *Mm*

machine

A **machine** is something with many parts for doing work.

mad

Mad means ill in the mind or very angry.

magazine

A **magazine** is a book with paper covers which comes every week or every month.

magic

Magic is the special power that makes strange things happen.

magnet

A **magnet** is a piece of iron that attracts iron towards it.

magnify • magnified

Magnify means to make things bigger.

make • made

Make means to create something.

man • men

A **man** is a grown-up male person.

many

Many means a large number of or a lot of.

map

A **map** is a drawing that shows where different places are.

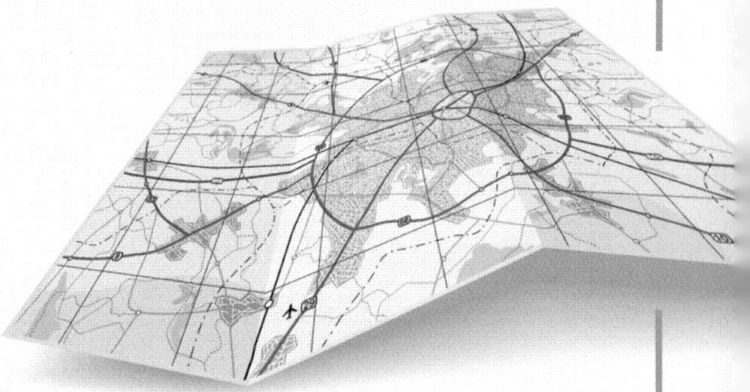

march

March means that all people walk together with the same steps.

mark

A **mark** is a spot or a line on something that spoils it.

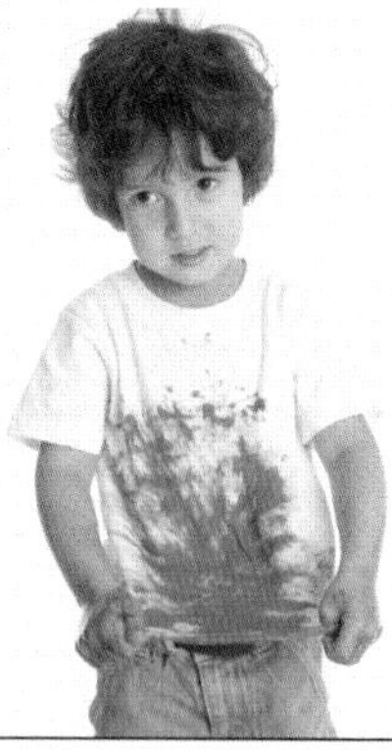

market

Lots of things are bought and sold at the **market**.

marry • married

Marry means to make someone your husband or wife.

meal

Breakfast, lunch, and dinner are **meals**.

measure

When we **measure** something, we find out the size of it or how much there is.

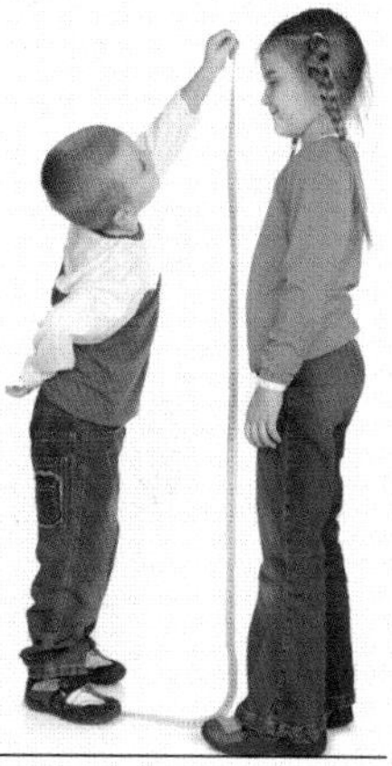

meat

Meat is the part of an animal that we eat.

medicine

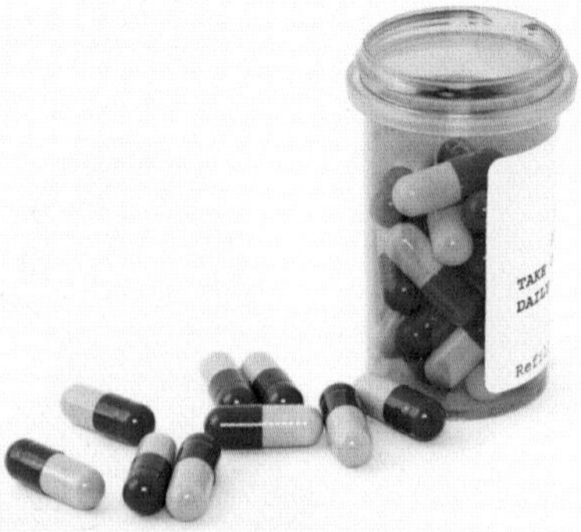

Medicine is something we take when we are sick.

meet • met

Meet means to come together with someone.

melt

When ice gets warm, it **melts** and becomes water.

microscope

A **microscope** can make tiny things look bigger.

middle

The **middle** is the part that is in the center.

milk

Milk is a white liquid that comes from cows.

minute

A **minute** is an amount of time equal to 60 seconds.

15 seconds **30** seconds
45 seconds **1** minute = **60** seconds

mirror

A **mirror** is a piece of glass you can see yourself in.

Miss

Miss is a word people use with a woman's name if she has not married.

mistake

A **mistake** is something that is wrong.

mitten

A **mitten** is a glove that covers the four fingers together and the thumb separately.

mix

If you put different things together, you **mix** them.

a b c d e f g h i j k l m n o p q r s t u v w x y z

model

A **model** is a small copy of a large object.

money

Money is what you use to buy something.

monkey

A **monkey** is a manlike animal with long arms and legs.

monster

A **monster** is a huge, frightening, evil thing.

month

A **month** is one of the twelve parts of a year.

moon

The **moon** is the object that shines in the sky at night.

more

More means a larger amount or number.

morning

Morning is the first part of the day.

mosquito

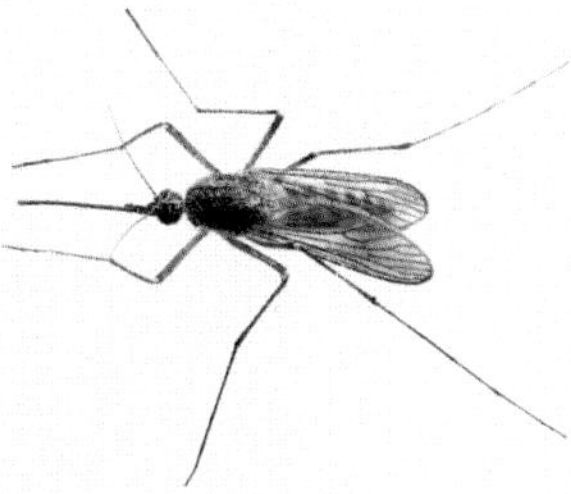

A **mosquito** is an insect that drinks blood from people or animals.

moth

A **moth** is an insect. **Moths** look like small butterflies, but their wings are not as pretty.

mother

A **mother** is a female parent.

motor

A **motor** uses electricity or gas to make a machine work.

mountain

A **mountain** is a very high hill.

mouse • mice

A **mouse** is a small animal. It has big ears, short fur, and a long tail.

mouth

You use your **mouth** to speak and eat.

move

Move means to go from one place to another.

movie

A **movie** is a story with moving pictures.

mud

Mud is very wet dirt.

muscle

A **muscle** is something that helps you move the parts of your body.

museum

A **museum** is a building where people can see beautiful and old things.

mushroom

A **mushroom** is a small, special kind of plant without leaves, shaped like an umbrella.

music

The pleasant sounds made by instruments or a person's voice are **music**.

Nn *Nn* Nn *Nn*

nap

A **nap** is a short sleep.

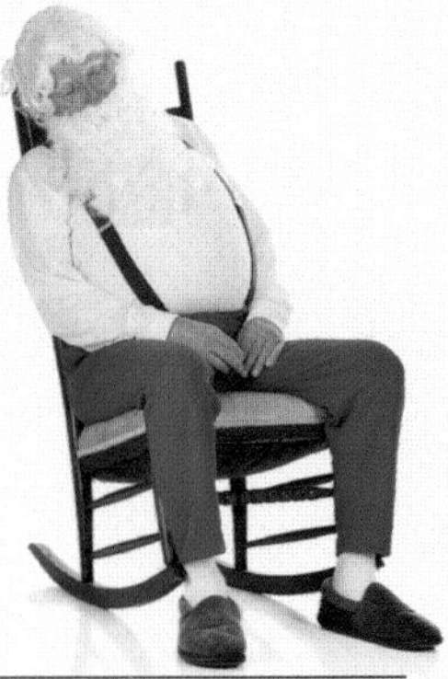

napkin

A **napkin** is a square piece of cloth or paper used at meals to clean your mouth and hands.

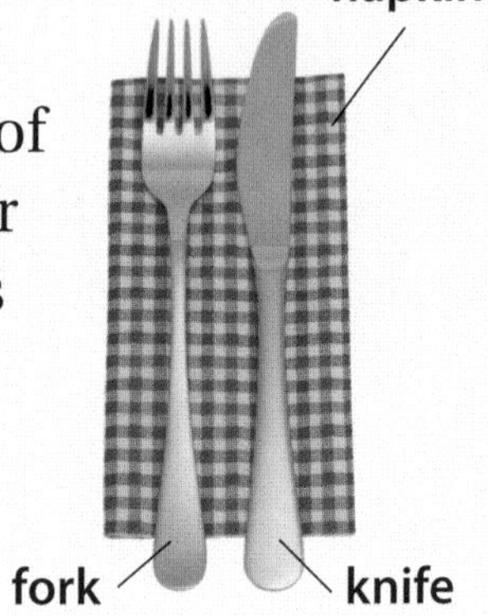

nail

A **nail** is a thin, pointed piece of metal.

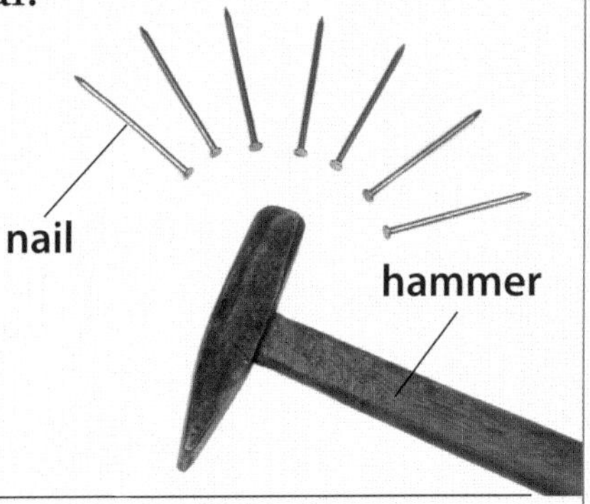

narrow

Narrow is the opposite of wide.

name

A **name** is what someone or something is called.

nature

People, animals, plants, sky, land, and water are all parts of **nature**.

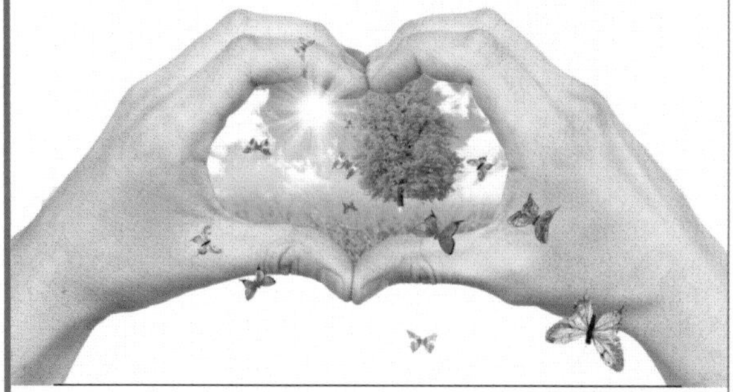

navy • navies

A **navy** is all the warships of a country.

near

Near means being close to something or someone.

neat

Neat means clean and tidy.

neck

The **neck** is the part of the body between the head and the shoulders.

needle

A **needle** is a thin, sharp-pointed tool for sewing.

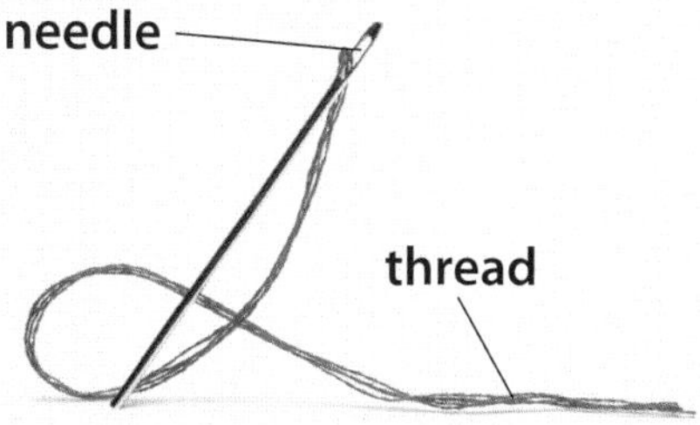

A B C D E F G H I J K L M N O P Q R S T U V W X Y Z

neighbor

A **neighbor** is somebody who lives near you.

nest

A **nest** is the home of some birds. It is made to hold eggs.

net

A **net** is used for catching fish, insects, or animals.

new

New means not old, used, or worn.

newspaper

A **newspaper** is a paper which has news, advertisements, and other information.

nice

Nice means pleasant or enjoyable.

night

Night is the opposite of day. **Night** begins when the sun sets. It ends when the sun rises.

no

No is the opposite of yes.

nobody

Nobody means no person.

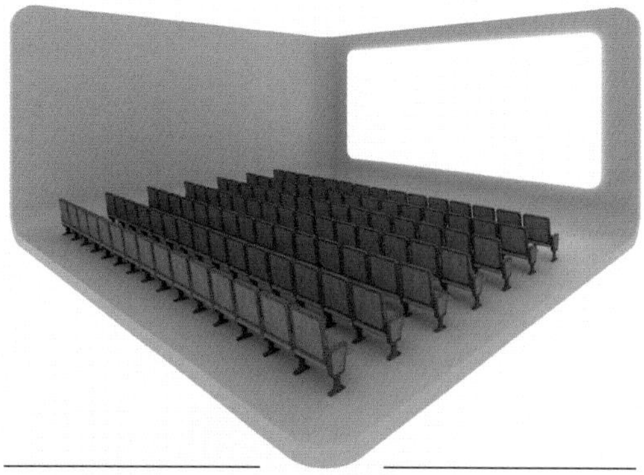

noise

A **noise** is a sound, often an unpleasant one.

noodle

Noodles are long, thin strips of pasta.

noon

Noon is a name for twelve o'clock. It is the middle of the day.

north

North is a direction. **North** is the opposite of south. If you look at where the sun rises, **north** is on your left.

nose

The **nose** is the part of the face that breathes and smells.

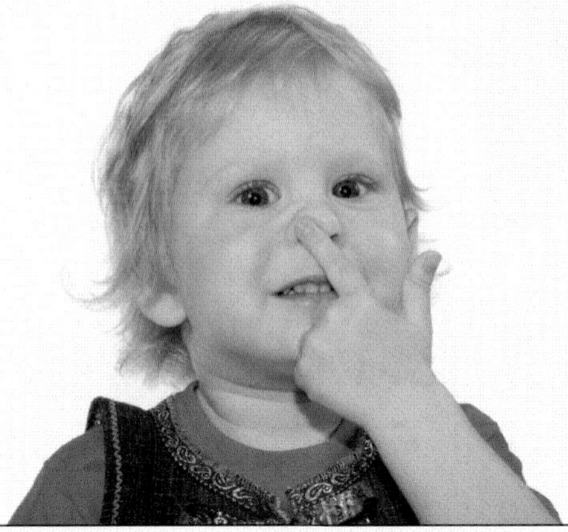

note

A **note** is a short, written message.

notebook

A **notebook** is a small book for writing notes in.

nothing

Nothing means there is not anything in a place.

number

A **number** is what we use when we count.

nurse

A **nurse** is a person who takes care of sick people.

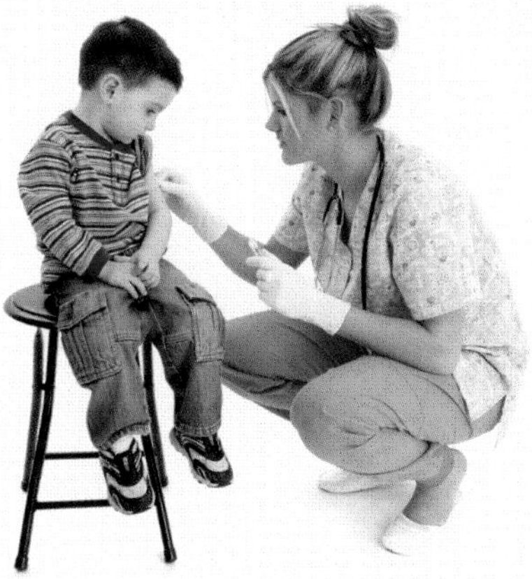

nut

A **nut** is a seed or a dry fruit.

Peanuts

Brazil nuts

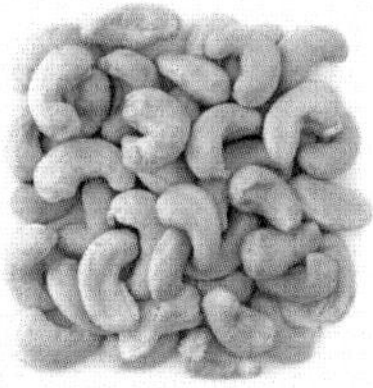
Cashew nuts

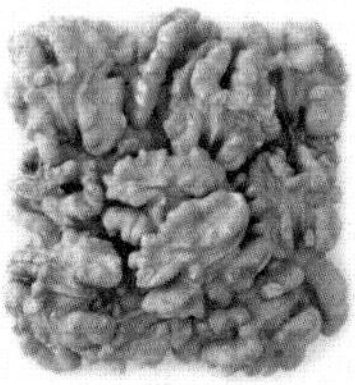
Walnuts

A B C D E F G H I J K L M N O P Q R S T U V W X Y Z

oasis • oases

An **oasis** is a small area in a desert where water and plants are found.

obey

When you **obey** somebody, you do what you are told to do.

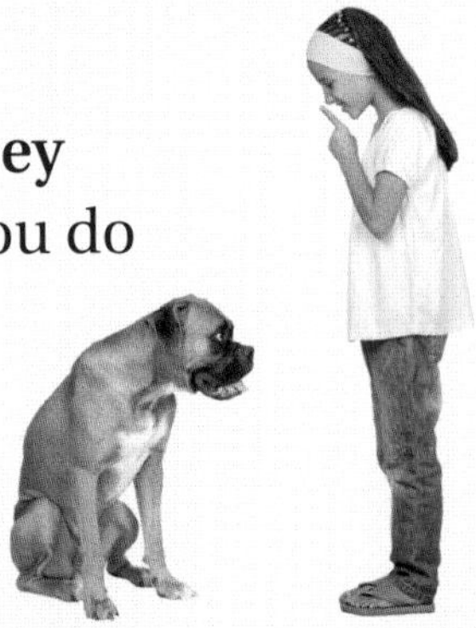

ocean

The **ocean** is the sea.

o'clock

O'clock is a word used to show an exact hour of the day.

three o'clock six o'clock

octopus

An **octopus** is an animal that lives in the sea. It has eight long arms.

office

An **office** is a place where people work.

often

Anything that happens again and again happens **often**.

oil

Oils from animals and vegetables are used in foods. **Oil** from the ground is used to make cars run.

OK

OK means all right.

old

An **old** person has lived for a long time.

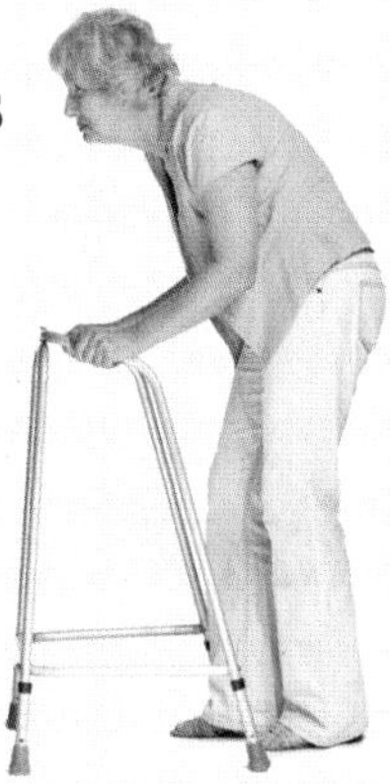

onion

An **onion** is a round vegetable. It has a strong smell and taste.

A B C D E F G H I J K L M N O P Q R S T U V W X Y Z

open

Open means not closed, so that things can go in and out.

opposite

Opposite means different in every way.

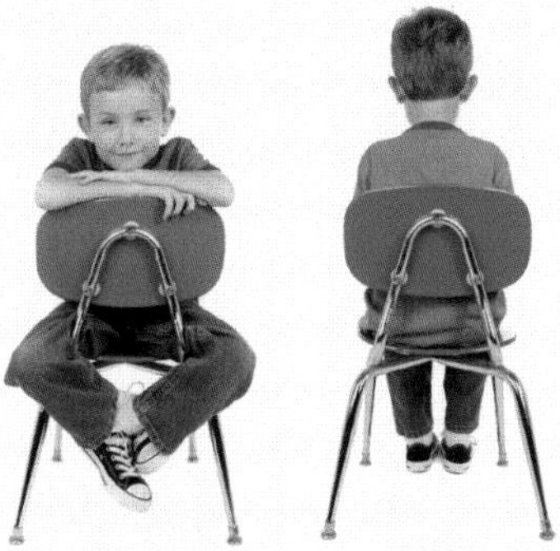

front back

orange

An **orange** is a round juicy fruit with a thick skin.

orchestra

An **orchestra** is a large group of people who play musical instruments together.

ostrich • ostriches

An **ostrich** is a large bird. It has long legs and a long neck. **Ostriches** cannot fly.

other

Other means different from the one or ones.

out

Out is the opposite of in.

oval

Anything **oval** is shaped like an egg.

oven

An **oven** is a metal box that food is cooked in.

owl

An **owl** is a bird with a flat face and large eyes.

ox • **oxen**

An **ox** is a male cow used for farm work.

a b c d e f g h i j k l m n o p q r s t u v w x y z

A B C D E F G H I J K L M N O P Q R S T U V W X Y Z

Pp *Pp* Pp *Pp*

pack

A **pack** is a large bag that you carry on your back.

package

A **package** is a box that you send in the mail.

page

A **page** is one side of a piece of paper.

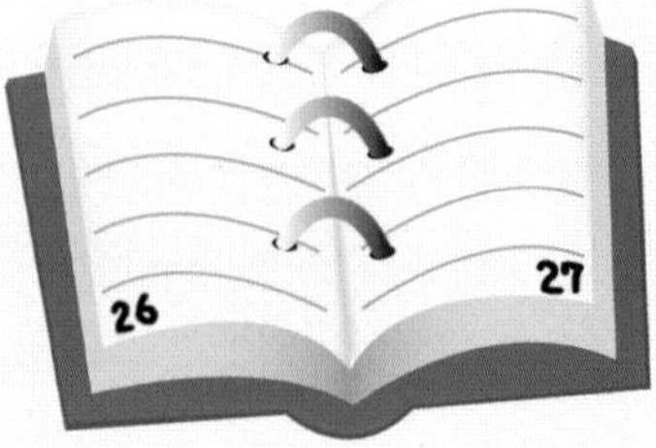

pail

A **pail** is a bucket, often used for carrying or holding water.

pain

Pain is the feeling you have when you are ill or hurt.

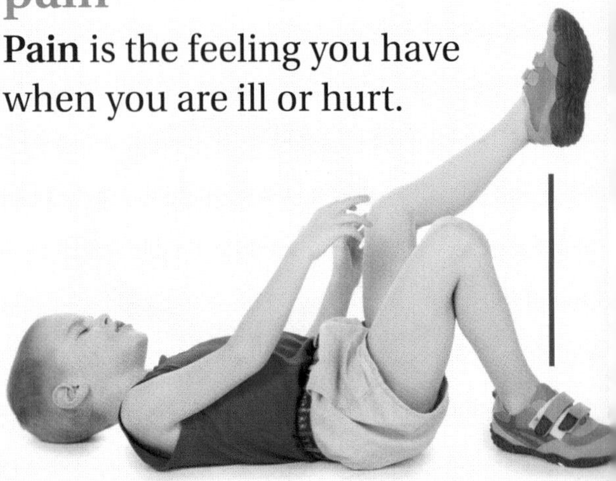

paint

Paint means to make a picture using **paints**.

pair

A **pair** is two things that go together.

pajamas

Pajamas are a kind of clothes. People wear them while they sleep.

pan

A **pan** is a round metal pot with a long handle for cooking.

pancake

A **pancake** is a very thin, flat cake made from flour, milk, and eggs.

paper

Paper is something you use to write on.

A B C D E F G H I J K L M N O P Q R S T U V W X Y Z

parade

A **parade** is a group of people, bands, or cars that follow each other on a street.

parent

A **parent** is the mother or the father of a child.

park

A **park** is an outside place where people walk or rest.

parrot

A **parrot** is a bird with brightly colored feathers. It has a large beak.

party • parties

A **party** is a group of people having fun.

pass

Pass means to hand something to someone.

passenger

A **passenger** is a person who is traveling in a car or train, but who is not working on it.

passport

You need your **passport** to travel from one country to another.

path

A **path** is a narrow piece of land for people to walk along.

patient

A **patient** is a person who is being looked after by a doctor.

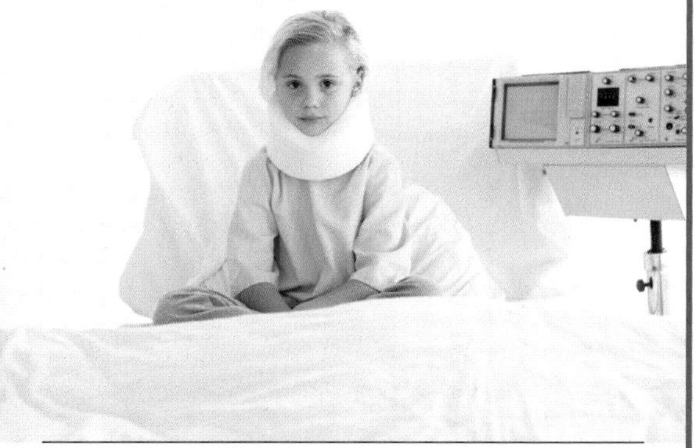

pattern

A **pattern** is the way colors and lines look on something.

paw

A **paw** is the foot of an animal.

A B C D E F G H I J K L M N O P Q R S T U V W X Y Z

pay • paid

Pay means to give money to someone for something.

peach • peaches

A **peach** is a round fruit with yellow and red skin and a pit inside.

peacock

A **peacock** is a large, male bird with beautiful feathers in its tail.

peanut

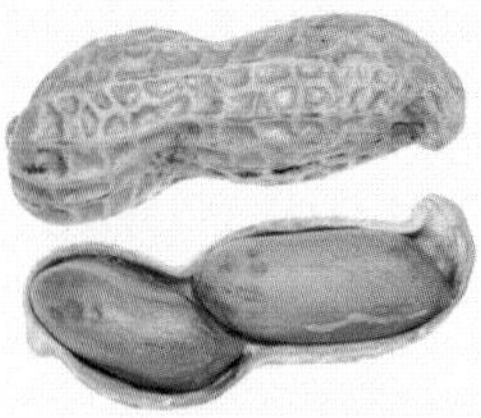

A **peanut** is a nut-like seed in a hard shell.

pear

A **pear** is a sweet, juicy, yellow or green fruit with a round shape.

pearl

If you are lucky, you may find a **pearl** in an oyster. You need lots of **pearls** to make a necklace.

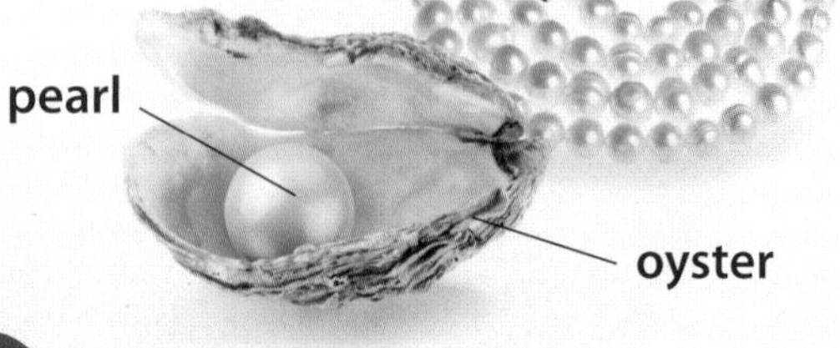

peel

The **peel** is the skin of some fruits and vegetables.

pen

A **pen** is a tool for writing. You use a **pen** for writing with ink.

pencil

A **pencil** is a writing tool made from wood.

pencil case

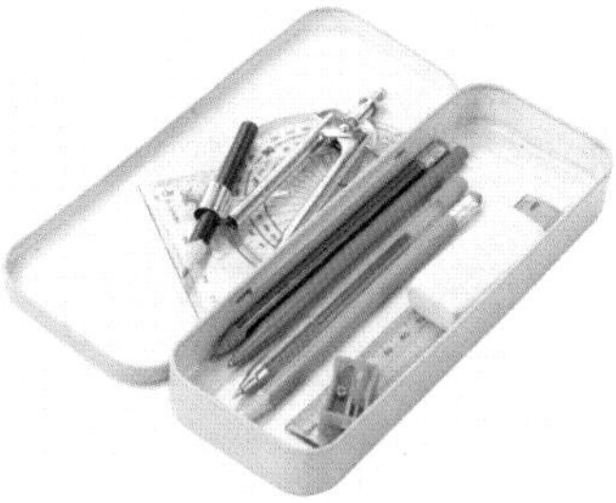

A **pencil case** is a small container for holding pencils and pens.

penguin

A **penguin** is a bird. It lives in very cold places near the ocean.

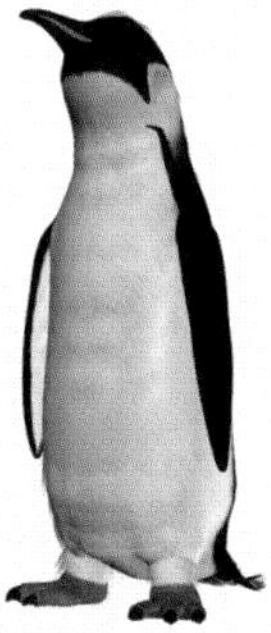

people

People are men, women, and children.

pepper

Pepper is a powder with a hot taste.

person

A **person** is a man, woman, or child.

pet

A **pet** is an animal that you keep in your home.

phone

A **phone** sends voices from one place to another. **Phone** is short for telephone.

piano

A **piano** is a large instrument played by pressing the keys.

pick
Pick means to take flowers or fruit from the plant or tree.

picnic

A **picnic** is a meal that people eat outside.

picture
A **picture** is something that you draw or take.

pie

A **pie** is a baked dish of fruit or meat.

piece
A **piece** is a part of something.

pig
A **pig** is an animal with a fat body and short legs.

A B C D E F G H I J K L M N O P Q R S T U V W X Y Z

pile
Things placed on top of each other are in a **pile**.

pill

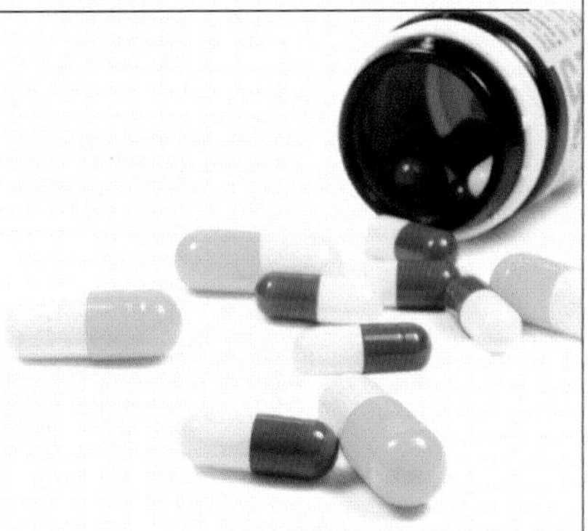

A **pill** is medicine made into a little ball or easy-to-swallow shape.

pillow
A **pillow** is something to put under your head when you sleep.

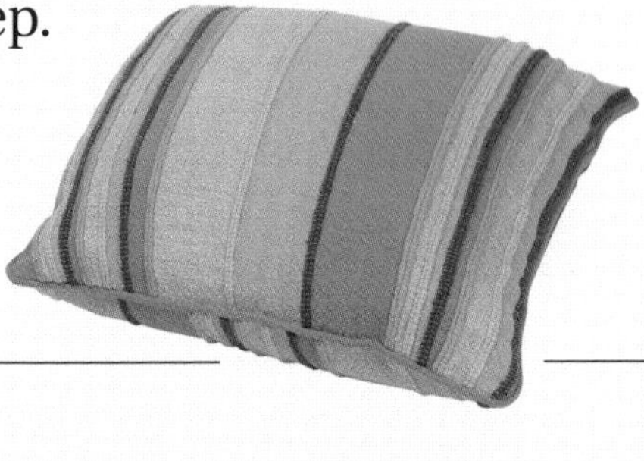

pilot
A **pilot** is a person who flies an airplane.

pin
A **pin** is a piece of metal. It is short, thin, and straight. It has a sharp point.

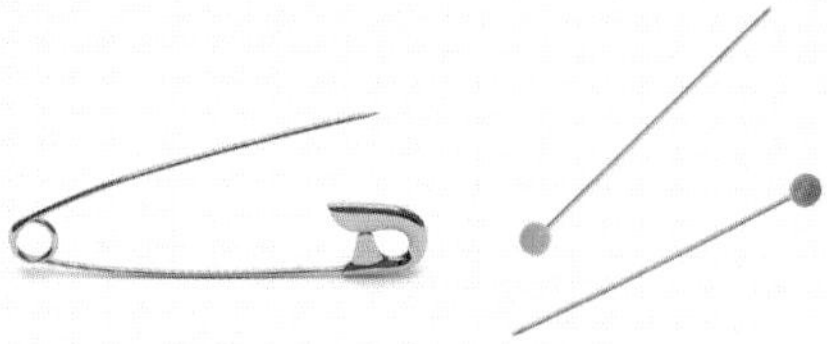

pipe
A **pipe** is a long tube that carries water.

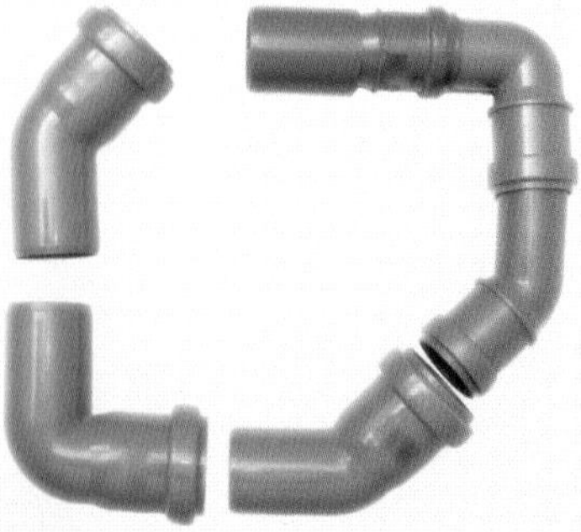

pirate

A **pirate** is a person who robs ships at sea.

plane

A **plane** is a vehicle that can fly in the air.

pizza

A **pizza** is a flat, round food that is baked in an oven.

planet

A **planet** is a big, round thing in space that moves around a star.

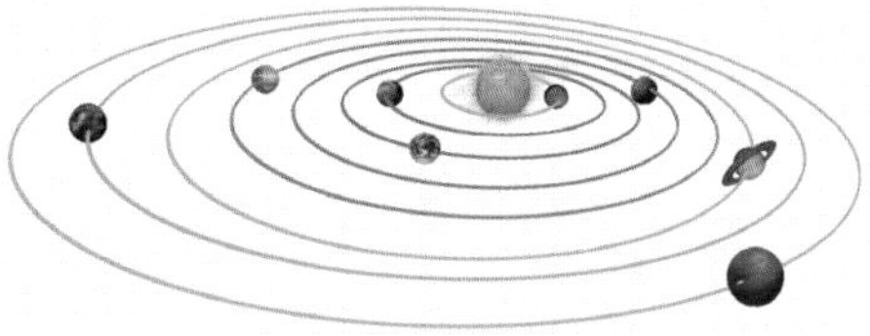

plan

A **plan** is a group of ideas about what to do.

plant

A **plant** is a living thing which usually grows in soil. It needs water and sunlight.

A B C D E F G H I J K L M N O P Q R S T U V W X Y Z

plastic

Many things are made from **plastic**. **Plastic** can be thin or thick. It can be soft or hard.

plate

A **plate** is a round, flat dish that you put food on.

play

Play means to do something for fun.

playground

A **playground** is an outdoor area where children can play.

plenty

If there is **plenty** of something, there is more than you need.

plus

Plus means that one number is added to another.

pocket

A **pocket** is a small bag of cloth.

point

A **point** is the thin, sharp end of something.

poison

Poison is something that can hurt or kill living things.

polar bear

A **polar bear** is a big, white bear that lives in very cold parts of the world in the north.

pole

A **pole** is a long piece of wood or metal.

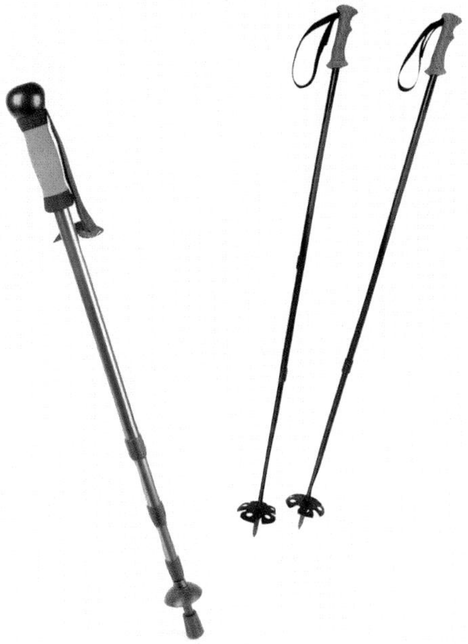

A
B
C
D
E
F
G
H
I
J
K
L
M
N
O
P
Q
R
S
T
U
V
W
X
Y
Z

police
The **police** are people who work to keep us safe.

polite
Polite means having good manners.

pollute
Pollute means to make something dirty.

pond
A **pond** is a kind of small lake.

pony • **ponies**
A **pony** is a small horse.

pool
A **pool** is an area filled with water for swimming.

poor

Poor is the opposite of rich. **Poor** people do not have much money.

popcorn

Popcorn is a kind of corn that opens with a pop when heated.

postman

A **postman** is a person whose job is to deliver mail.

post office

A **post office** is a building where you can buy stamps and send letters and packages.

pot

A **pot** is a deep, round container used for cooking.

potato • potatoes

A **potato** is a vegetable that grows under the ground.

pound

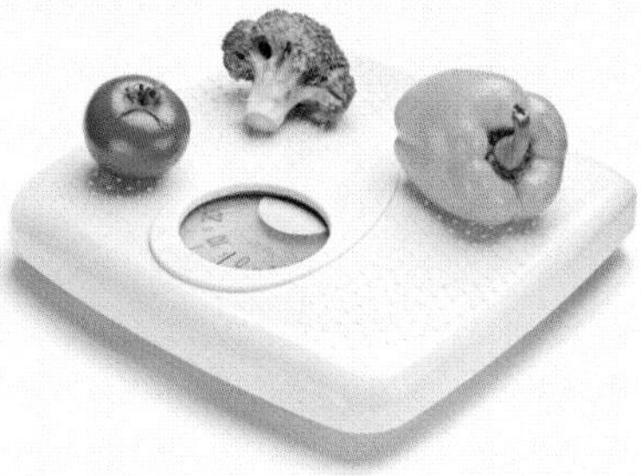

A **pound** is an amount of weight. It is about the same as 450 grams.

pour

Pour means to make a liquid flow out of a container.

pray

Pray means to ask God for help.

present

A **present** is a gift to give or to receive.

president

A **president** is a person that other people have chosen to lead a country.

Abraham Lincoln

press

Press means to push hard on something.

pretty

Pretty means nice to look at.

price

The **price** of something is how much money you have to pay for it.

prince

A **prince** is the son of a king or queen.

print

Print means to put letters or pictures onto paper using a machine.

prize

A **prize** is something that people win for doing well.

problem

A **problem** is always difficult to solve.

program

A **program** is a show that you watch on television.

promise

When you **promise**, you say that you will or will not do something.

propeller

When **propellers** turn, they make planes and boats move.

protect

Protect means to keep someone or something safe from harm.

proud

Proud means feeling good about something you have done.

prove

Prove means to show that something is true.

pull

Pull means to hold something and move it toward you.

pumpkin

A **pumpkin** is a large, orange vegetable with a thick skin.

punch

Punch means to make a hole in something.

punish

Punish means to make somebody sorry because they have done something wrong.

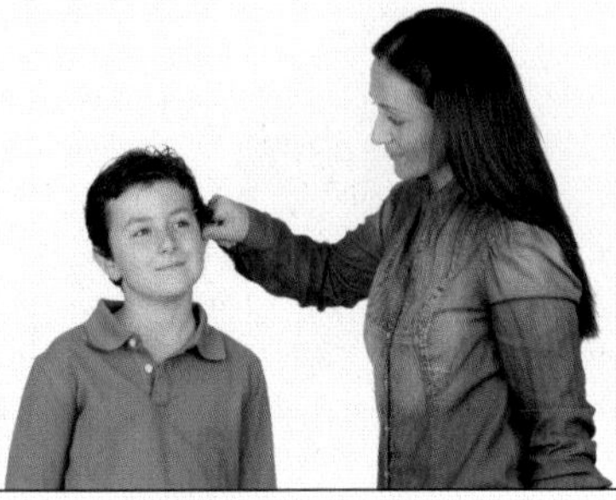

pupil

A **pupil** is a child who goes to a school.

puppet

A **puppet** is a kind of toy. It looks like a person or an animal. It is moved by strings.

puppy • **puppies**

A **puppy** is a young dog.

purse

A **purse** is a small bag or case for carrying money.

push

Push means to use your hands to move something away from you.

queen

A **queen** is a woman who rules a country.

quarrel

If you **quarrel** with someone, you get angry and argue.

quarter

A **quarter** is one of four equal parts.

question

You ask a **question** to find out something.

a b c d e f g h i j k l m n o p q r s t u v w x y z

A B C D E F G H I J K L M N O P Q R S T U V W X Y Z

quick
Quick means fast or speedy.

quiet
To be **quiet** is to be silent and make no noise at all.

quilt

A **quilt** is a cover or blanket of small pieces of cloth that have been sewn together.

quiz • quizzes
A **quiz** is like a test. You must answer a lot of questions.

MFE-D-r

Rr *Rr* Rr *Rr*

rabbit

A **rabbit** is a small, short-tailed animal with long ears.

race

A **race** is any contest to find which person or animal is the fastest.

radio

A **radio** is a machine you can turn on and listen to.

railroad

A **railroad** is the metal path that trains ride on.

rain

Rain is drops of water that come down from the sky.

A B C D E F G H I J K L M N O P Q R S T U V W X Y Z

rainbow

A **rainbow** is like a ribbon of many colors. Sometimes **rainbows** appear in the sky.

raincoat

A **raincoat** is a coat that keeps you dry in the rain.

rake

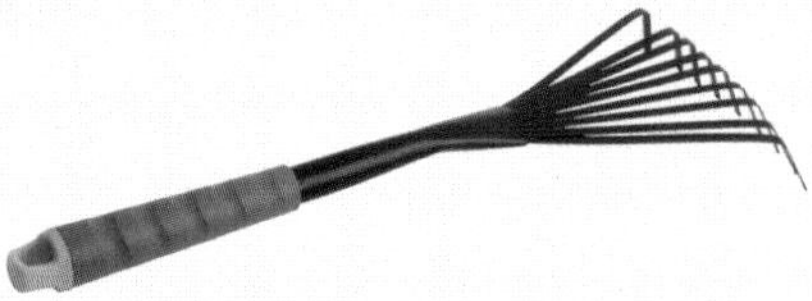

A **rake** is used for gathering fallen leaves or making soil smooth.

rat

A **rat** is an animal that looks like a big mouse.

reach

Reach means to stretch your hand towards something.

read • **read**

Read means to get the meaning of written words.

ready

Ready means that you can do something without waiting any longer.

receive

Receive means to get something.

record

Record means to keep words, sounds, or images for later.

referee

A **referee** makes sure the players keep to the rules of the game.

refrigerator

A **refrigerator** is a machine that keeps food cold and fresh.

refuse

If you **refuse**, you say you will not do something that somebody has asked you to do.

A B C D E F G H I J K L M N O P Q R S T U V W X Y Z

repair

Repair means to fix something.

rescue

If you save a person from danger, you **rescue** them.

rest

Rest means to relax. When you feel tired, sit down and **rest**.

restaurant

A **restaurant** is a place where you can eat a meal and pay for it.

return

Return means to go back or come back from somewhere.

ribbon

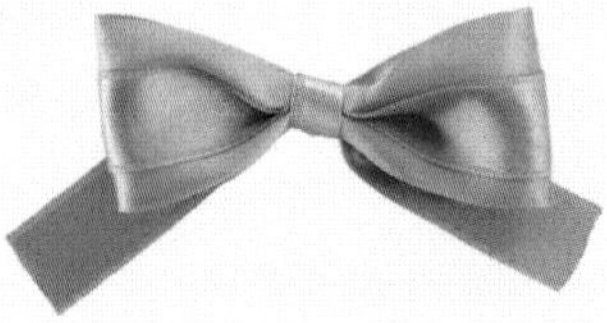

A **ribbon** is a piece of cloth or paper. It is long and thin.

rice
Rice is a grain. It grows in fields flooded with water.

ring
A **ring** is a small circle of metal that you wear around your finger.

rich

Rich is the opposite of poor. **Rich** people have a lot of money.

river
Rivers begin in the hills as small streams. They grow deeper and wider and then flow into the sea.

ride • rode, ridden
Ride means to sit on something and control it.

road
A **road** is a way on which people and vehicles travel.

rob • robbed

Rob means to take something that does not belong to you.

robot

A **robot** is a machine. It can do some of the jobs people can do.

rock

Rock is the very hard material that mountains are made of.

rocket

A **rocket** is a big machine for traveling into space. Astronauts travel through space in a **rocket**.

roll

Roll means to move by turning over and over.

roof

A **roof** is the part on top that covers a building or something like a car or a bus.

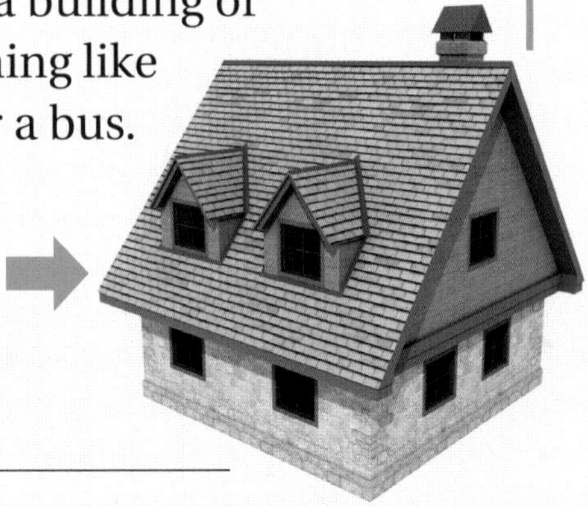

room

A **room** is a part of a building with a floor, walls, and a ceiling.

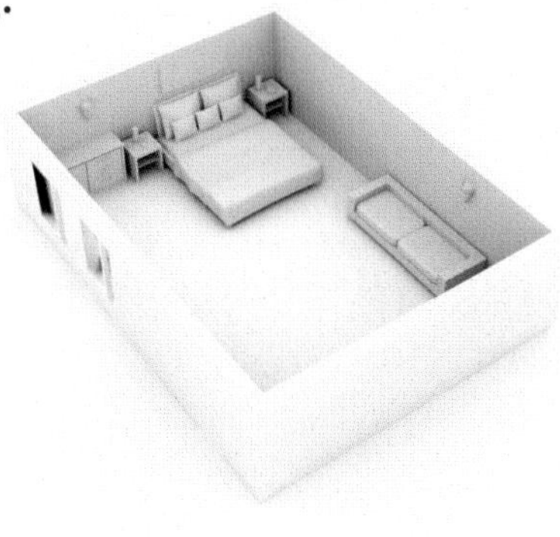

root

A **root** is a part of a plant growing under the ground.

rope

A **rope** is used to tie things. It is made of several strings twisted together.

rose

A **rose** is a sweet-smelling flower with thorny stems.

round

Round means shaped like a circle or a ball.

A B C D E F G H I J K L M N O P Q R S T U V W X Y Z

rub • **rubbed**

When you **rub** something, you move your hand or another thing backward and forward across it.

rubber

Rubber is a strong material that can stretch but doesn't break.

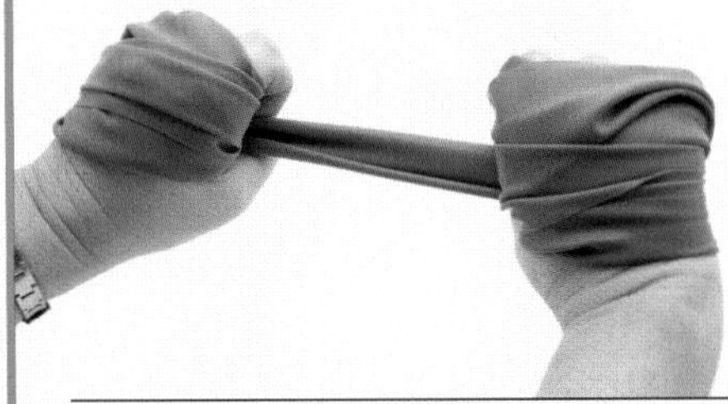

rude

If you are **rude** to someone, you are not polite or friendly to them.

rug

A **rug** is used to cover part of a floor. It is made of wool or other things.

ruler

A **ruler** is a piece of wood, metal, or plastic that you use for drawing or measuring straight lines.

run • **ran, run**

Run means to move your legs quickly to travel faster than walking.

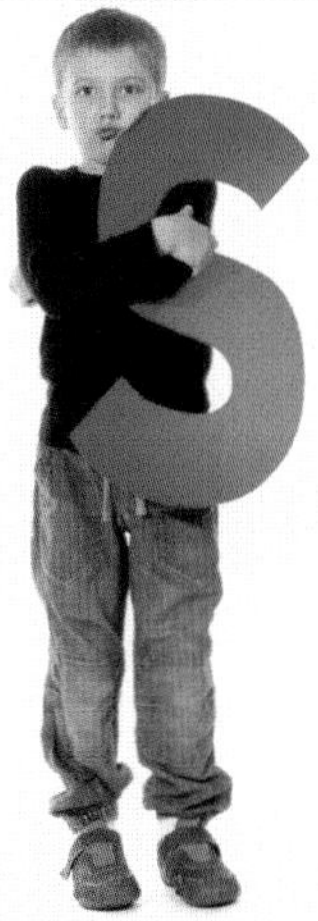

Ss Ss Ss Ss

sail

A **sail** is a large piece of strong cloth. **Sails** are tied to tall poles on boats.

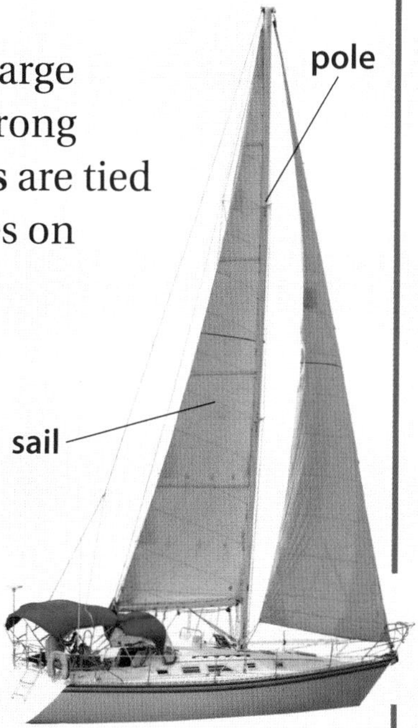

sad

Sad means feeling unhappy about something.

safe

Safe means not being in any danger.

salad

A **salad** is a cold food made of different vegetables and fruit mixed together.

salt

Salt is a white powder used in cooking.

a b c d e f g h i j k l m n o p q r s t u v w x y z

same

Same is the opposite of different. These twins look the **same**.

sand

Sand is very small pieces of stone. **Sand** is found on beaches and in deserts.

sandwich • **sandwiches**

To make a **sandwich**, you put your favorite food between two slices of bread.

school

A **school** is a building where students learn.

science

Science uses experiments and careful testing to learn things and discover facts.

scissors

Scissors have two sharp blades fixed in the middle. They can cut paper, cloth and even your hair.

sculptor

A **sculptor** makes objects by cutting away from a block of material, such as stone or wood. These objects are called sculptures.

sea

The **sea** is the salt water that covers most of the Earth.

search

When you **search** for something, you look very carefully for it.

season

There are four **seasons**. Each one is a quarter of a year.

second

Second means coming just after the first thing or person.

secret

A **secret** is something hidden or unknown.

sell • sold

Sell means to give something in exchange for money.

seed

A **seed** is a part of a plant that can grow in soil.

send • sent

Send means to make something go from one place to another.

seesaw

Seesaws are found in parks for children to play on. One end of the **seesaw** goes up while the other goes down.

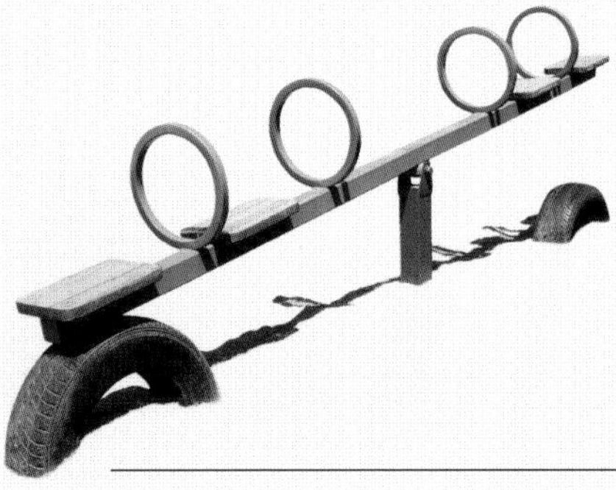

serve

Serve means to give people food or drink.

set

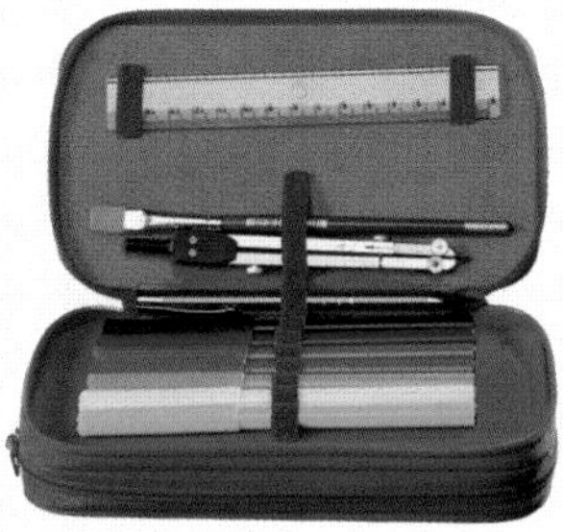

A **set** means a group of similar things together in one place.

sew • sewed, sewn

A needle, thread, and a piece of cloth is all you need to **sew**.

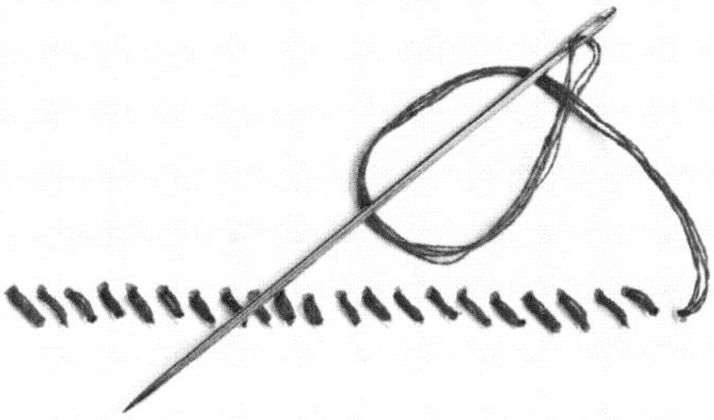

shadow

When the sun is shining, your **shadow** goes everywhere with you.

shake • shook, shaken

Shake means to move something up and down or from side to side.

shape

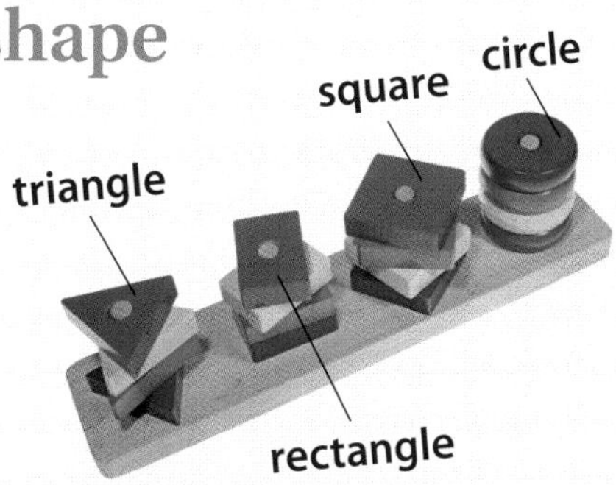

Circles, squares and triangles are **shapes**.

share

If you **share** something with another person, you both have it or use it.

a b c d e f g h i j k l m n o p q r s t u v w x y z

sharp

Something is **sharp** if it has a point or thin edge that can cut. Knives have **sharp** edges.

sheep • **sheep**

A **sheep** is an animal with a thick coat of wool.

shell

A **shell** is the hard outside part of an egg, a nut or an animal.

shine • **shone**

Shine means to give off bright light.

ship

A **ship** is a big boat. **Ships** carry people and things across the ocean.

shirt

You wear a **shirt** on the top part of your body.

shoe
A **shoe** is something that covers a foot. It may be made of leather, plastic, or cloth.

shoot • shot
Shoot means to fire a gun or other weapon.

shop
A **shop** is a place where people can buy things.

shore
The **shore** is the land along the edge of a lake or an ocean.

short
Short is the opposite of tall or long. Which pencil is **shorter**?

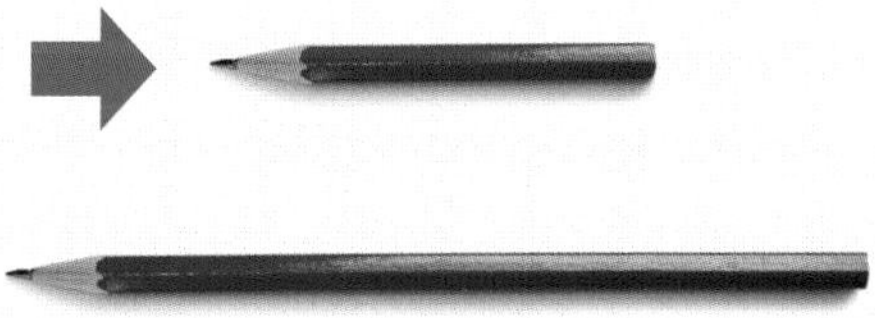

show • **showed, shown**

When you **show** something, you let people see it.

shower

A **shower** is the act of washing your body with a spray of water.

shut • **shut**

When a thing is **shut**, it is closed, not open.

shy

Shy means nervous about meeting or speaking to other people.

sick

Sick means not feeling well.

side

A **side** is one of the surfaces of an object.

sign

A **sign** is a mark or letter that expresses an idea.

silly

Silly means not serious. If someone is being **silly**, they are acting foolishly.

silver

Silver is a grayish-white, shiny metal.

sing • sang, sung

You make music with your voice when you **sing** a song.

single

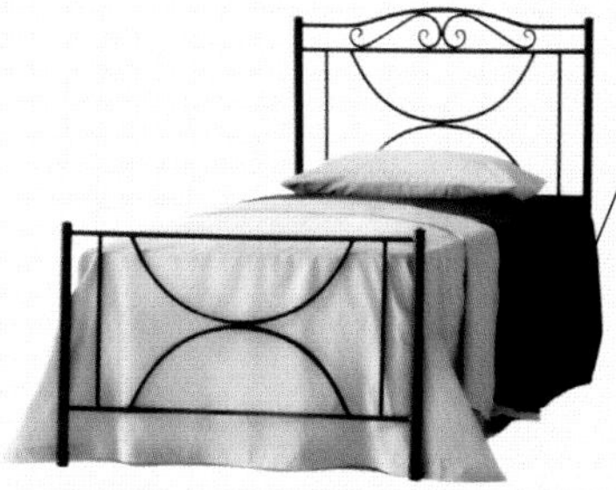

Single means only one or suitable for one person only.

sink • sank, sunk

Sink means to go below the surface of the water.

a b c d e f g h i j k l m n o p q r s t u v w x y z

sister

Your **sister** is a girl who has the same parents as you.

sit • sat

Sit means to rest on the bottom part of the body.

size

The **size** of something is how big it is.

ski

A **ski** is a long piece of wood, metal, or plastic used to move across snow.

skin

Your **skin** is the natural covering of your body.

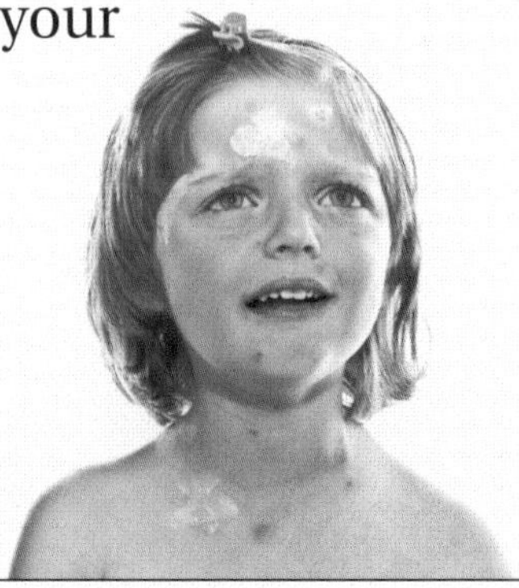

sky

The **sky** is up above you. It can be blue in the day, black at night, and sometimes grey and cloudy.

sleep • slept

Sleep means to rest with your eyes closed.

slide

A **slide** is a piece of playground equipment that has a slope.

slip • slipped

Slip means to slide and fall down.

slow

When something is **slow**, it is not moving quickly.

small

Small means little and not very big.

A B C D E F G H I J K L M N O P Q R S T U V W X Y Z

smell

Smell means to give off an odor.

smile

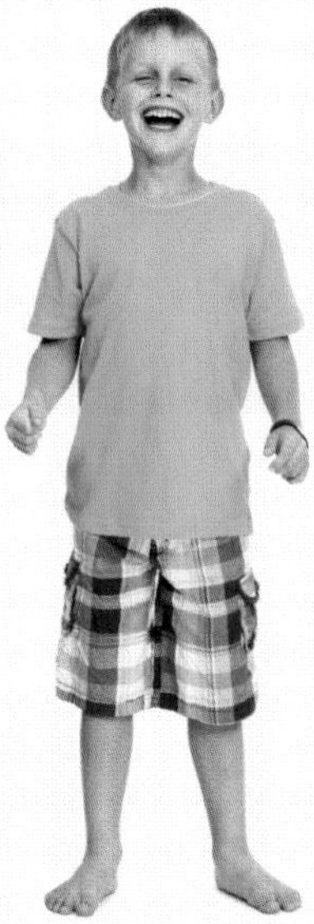

You **smile** and look happy when you are pleased.

smoke

Smoke is made by burning something. **Smoke** can be black, grey, or white and looks like a cloud.

smooth

If something is **smooth**, you cannot feel any rough parts on it.

snail

A **snail** is a small creature with a hard shell on its back.

snake

A **snake** is a long, thin, crawling animal without legs.

snow

Snow is soft white pieces of frozen water that fall from the sky in cold weather.

soap

A good wash with **soap** and water makes the dirt disappear.

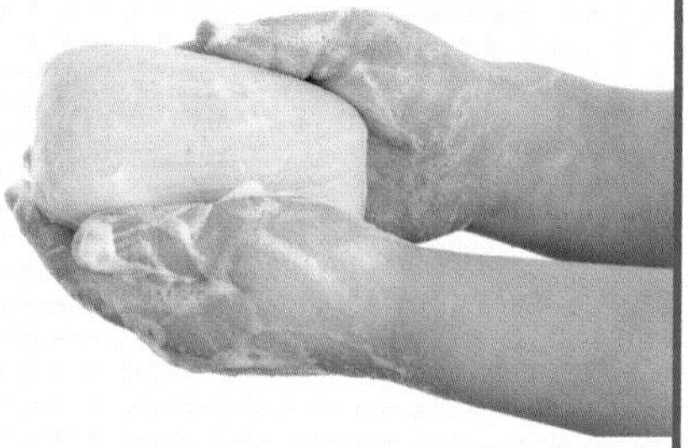

sock

A **sock** is a kind of clothes. People wear **socks** over their feet and under their shoes.

sofa

A **sofa** is a long, comfortable seat for more than one person.

soft

Fur and feathers are **soft** to touch, not hard at all.

soil

Soil is the top part of the ground.

soldier

A **soldier** is a person who works in an army.

some

Some means a certain amount or number of.

son

A **son** is a person's male child.

song

A **song** is music that someone sings. Some **songs** use both instruments and voices together.

soon

Soon means before long.

sorry

Sorry means feeling regret for something.

sound

A **sound** is something that you can hear.

soup

Soup is a liquid food made from meat, vegetables, etc.

sour

Sour means having a taste like the taste of a lemon.

south

South is the point opposite to north. If you look at where the sun rises, **south** is on your right.

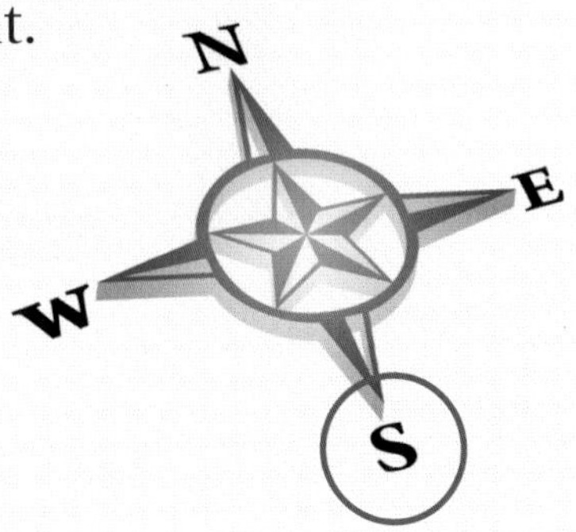

space

Space is the sky around the Earth and farther away where all the stars and planets are.

speak • spoke, spoken

People use their voices to talk. They **speak** words.

special

Special means different from normal. Singers wear **special** clothes on the stage.

spell

Spell means to put the letters of a word in the right order.

spend • spent

Spend means to use your money or time to do something.

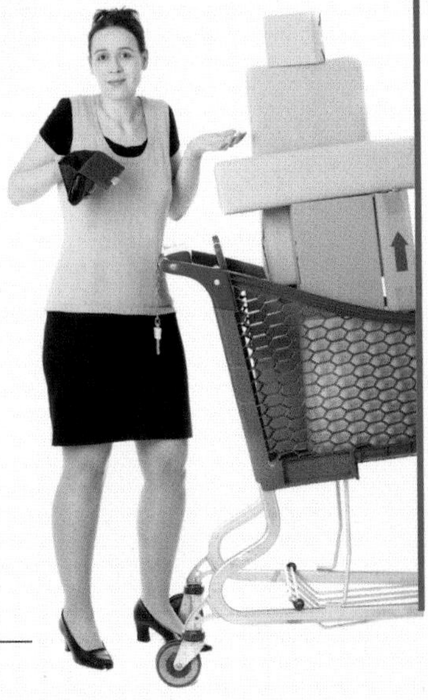

spider

A **spider** is a very small animal with eight legs and no wings.

spill

If you **spill** something, you make it flow out by mistake.

spoon

A **spoon** is a kind of tool to eat with. It looks like a tiny metal bowl joined to a handle.

spring

Spring is the season between winter and summer when plants start to grow.

stair

Stairs are steps for going up and down.

stamp

A **stamp** is a small piece of paper. People use **stamps** to pay for letters or packages they send through the mail.

a b c d e f g h i j k l m n o p q r s t u v w x y z

star

You can see **stars** at night as small points of light in the sky.

start

Start means to begin something.

station

Travelers on trains and buses arrive and depart at the **station**.

statue

A **statue** is the shape of a person or an animal made of stone or metal.

stay

Stay means not to leave a place.

steal • stole, stolen

Steal means to take things that don't belong to you.

steam

When water boils, it turns into a misty cloud called **steam**.

step

A **step** is the act of lifting your foot and putting it down.

stone

A **stone** is a small piece of rock. Smooth **stones** are found on seashores.

stop • stopped

If you **stop** doing something, you don't continue your action.

store

A **store** is a place where things are sold.

a b c d e f g h i j k l m n o p q r s t u v w x y z

A B C D E F G H I J K L M N O P Q R S T U V W X Y Z

storm

Thunder, lightning, wind, and rain all add up to a **storm**.

story • stories

A **story** tells about what happened to people and places.

straight

Straight means not bent or curved.

strange

Something that is **strange** is very different from what you expect.

straw

A **straw** is a long, thin tube made of paper or plastic for drinking.

street

A **street** is a road with houses and shops on both sides.

stretch

If you **stretch** a thing, it gets longer or wider.

stripe

Stripes are lines of different colors.

strong

Strong means powerful. **Strong** is the opposite of weak.

student

A **student** is a person who is studying at a school. One class has many **students** in it.

submarine

A **submarine** is a boat that can travel under water.

sudden

Sudden means quick and unexpected.

sugar

Sugar makes things sweet. It is something people put on food and in drinks.

suit

A jacket and pants made from the same material are a **suit**.

summer

Summer is the warmest season of the year. We hope it is hot on our **summer** holidays.

sun

The **sun** is a kind of star. We see it shine in the sky during the day. The **sun** gives us heat and light.

supermarket
A **supermarket** is a big store where food is sold.

surprise
If you don't expect something to happen, it comes as a **surprise**.

sweet
Sweet means tasting like sugar or honey.

swim • swam, swum

Swim means to move in the water by using your arms and legs.

MFE-D-t

Tt *Tt* Tt *Tt*

take • took, taken

When you **take** something, you hold it with your hands.

talk

When people speak words, they **talk**.

table

A **table** is a piece of furniture with a flat top and legs.

tall

Tall is the opposite of short.

tail

A **tail** is the part at the end of an animal's body.

taste

We **taste** bitter, sweet, and sour flavors with our tongue.

taxi

A **taxi** is a car with a driver that people pay to ride in.

tea

Tea is a drink made by adding hot water to tea leaves or tea bags.

teach • taught

Teach means to give lessons to someone.

teacher

A **teacher** helps students to understand many things.

team

A **team** is a group of people who work or play together.

A B C D E F G H I J K L M N O P Q R S T U V W X Y Z

tear

A **tear** is a drop of salty water coming from the eyes.

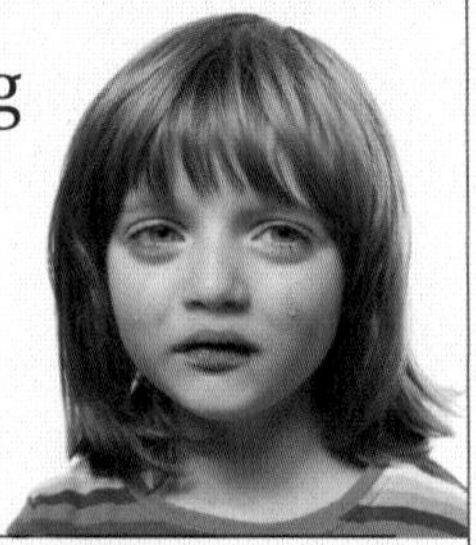

telephone

You can speak to someone far away on a **telephone**.

telescope

When you look through a **telescope**, you can see a long way. Its lenses make things look bigger and nearer.

television

A **television** gives us pictures and sounds from signals sent through the air from a long distance.

tell • **told**

Tell means to say something to someone.

temperature

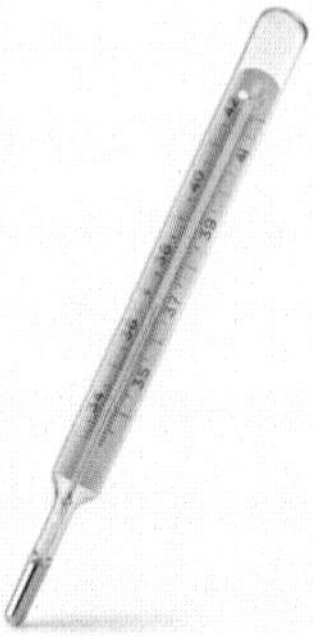

The **temperature** of something is how hot or cold it is.

tennis

Tennis is a game played by hitting a ball over a net with a racket.

tent

A **tent** is a place to sleep in that is made of cloth and held up by poles and ropes.

test

A **test** is a way to find out how much you know about something.

thank

If you are grateful for something, you say **thank** you.

theater

A **theater** is a place to watch movies or plays.

thick

Something that is **thick** measures a lot from one side to the other.

a b c d e f g h i j k l m n o p q r s t u v w x y z

thin

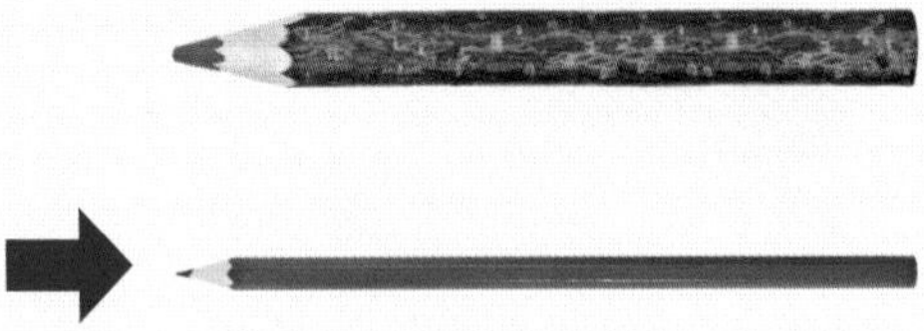

Thin is the opposite of thick.

think · thought

When you **think**, you are using your brain.

third

Third means next after the second one.

thirsty

To be **thirsty** is to want a drink.

this

This is the thing or person near in time or space.

thorn

Thorns are the sharp points on some plants.

throat

Your **throat** is the part at the back of your mouth.

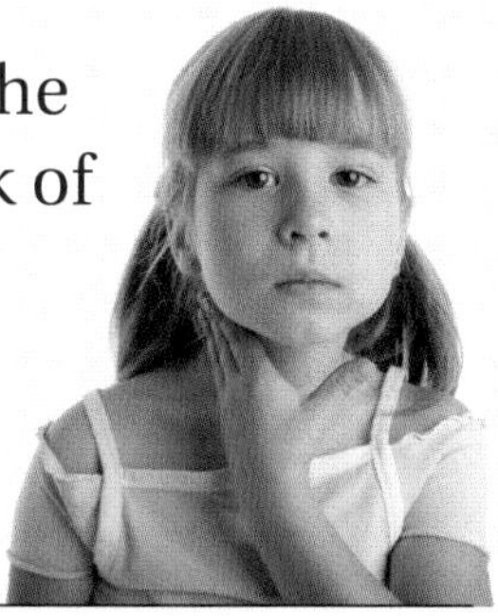

through

Through means from one side to the other.

throw • threw, thrown

When you **throw** something, you make it move through the air away from you.

thumb

The **thumb** is the short, thick finger on your hand.

thunder

Thunder is a loud sound in the sky that comes after lightning.

ticket

A **ticket** shows how much you paid to go somewhere.

tie

Tie means to bind something with a string, rope, etc.

tiger

A **tiger** is a big, wild animal that has orange and white fur with dark stripes.

tight

Tight is the opposite of loose.

timber

Timber is wood which has been cut into pieces ready to use in building.

time

Time measures how long things take.

tiny

Tiny means very small.

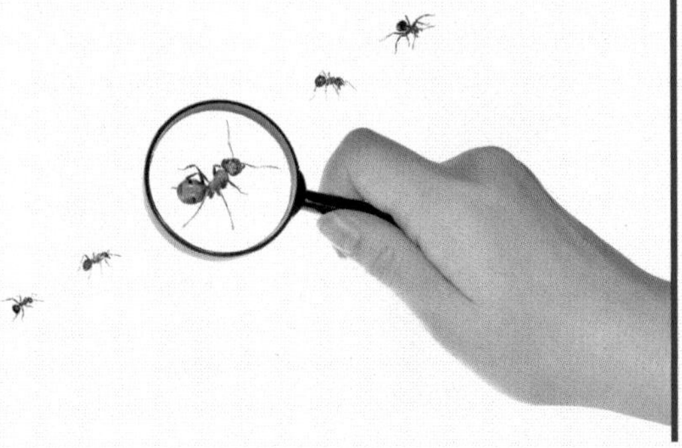

tire

A **tire** is a circle of rubber. It covers the outside of a wheel.

tired

Tired means feeling that you need to rest or sleep.

toad

A **toad** is an animal that looks like a large frog.

toast

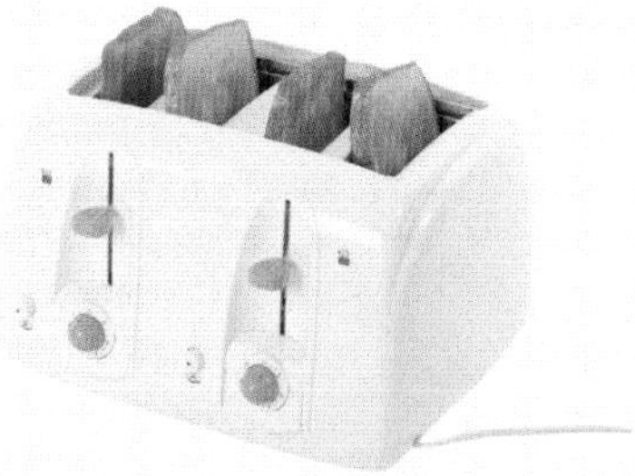

Toast is a slice of bread made brown on both sides by heat.

toe

A **toe** is a part of the foot. People have five **toes** on each foot.

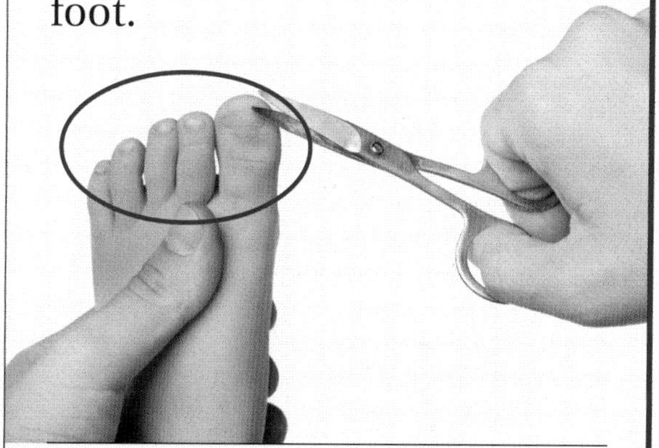

together

Together means with each other.

a b c d e f g h i j k l m n o p q r s t u v w x y z

tomato • tomatoes

A **tomato** is a round, red fruit that is filled with juice and seeds.

tongue

The **tongue** is the soft part in the mouth used for tasting and speaking.

tool

A **tool** is an object used to help you do work.

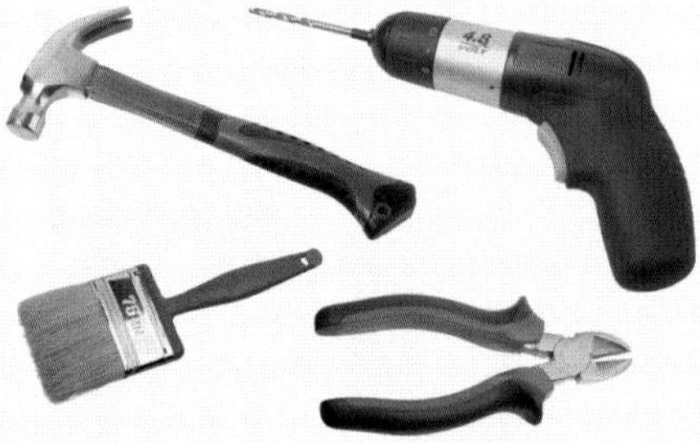

tooth • teeth

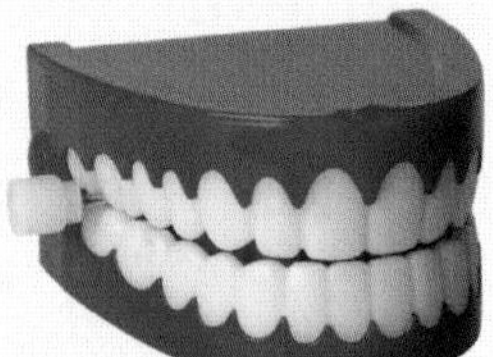

A **tooth** is one of the hard, white parts in your mouth. You bite and chew with your **teeth**.

toothbrush

A **toothbrush** is a small brush for cleaning your teeth.

top

The highest point of anything is the **top**. **Top** is the opposite of bottom.

touch

Touch means to put your hand on something.

tourist

A **tourist** is a person who is visiting a place for pleasure.

towel

A **towel** is used for drying or wiping something.

tower

A **tower** is a tall, high, narrow building or just part of one.

town

A **town** is full of people, streets, shops, and houses. It is not as big as a city.

toy

A **toy** is something to play with.

A B C D E F G H I J K L M N O P Q R S T U V W X Y Z

tractor

A **tractor** pulls farm machinery and moves heavy loads.

traffic

When there are many cars, trucks, and buses on the streets, there is a lot of **traffic**.

train

The **train** is a form of public transportation provided by a line of railway cars.

trash

Trash is things that you throw away.

travel

Travel means to go from one place to another over a long distance.

treasure

Gold, silver, and jewels are all kinds of **treasure**.

trick

A **trick** is something that seems impossible.

tree

A **tree** lives longer than any other plant. It has a trunk, branches, and leaves.

truck

A **truck** is a big vehicle for carrying goods.

triangle

A **triangle** is a shape with three sides joined.

trumpet

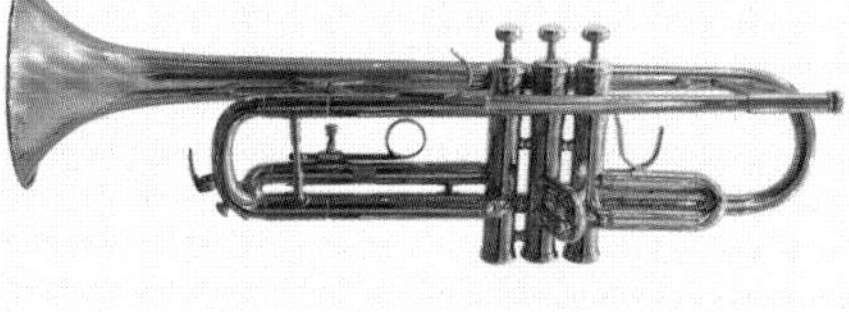

A **trumpet** is a musical instrument made of a curved metal tube.

try • tried

Try means to attempt.

tunnel

A **tunnel** is a long hole dug underground. Roads or railroads often go through **tunnels**.

turtle

A **turtle** is an animal. It is a reptile that lives both in the water and on land.

twin

A **twin** is one of two children born at the same time to the same mother.

Uu *Uu* Uu *Uu*

uncle

Any brother of your mother or your father is your **uncle**.

ugly

Somebody or something that is **ugly** is not nice to look at.

under

Under means lower than the bottom of something.

umbrella

An **umbrella** is an object people use when it rains. **Umbrellas** cover people and keep them dry.

understand • understood

If you **understand** something, you know what it means.

a b c d e f g h i j k l m n o p q r s t **u** v w x y z

underwear

Underwear is clothing that you wear under other clothes.

undress

Undress means to take off your clothes.

unhappy

Unhappy means not happy.

unicorn

A **unicorn** is a fairy tale animal with the body of a horse and a horn on its head.

uniform

Uniforms are the special sets of clothes worn by the same kind of people.

universe

Our world, the sun, the moon, and the stars are all parts of the **universe**.

untidy

If you describe something as **untidy**, you mean that it is not neat or well arranged.

up

Up is the opposite of down. To go **up** is to rise.

upstairs

Upstairs means to a higher floor of a building.

use

Use means to do something with a machine or an object.

vacant

Vacant means empty and not being used.

valley

A **valley** is the land between mountains or hills.

van

A **van** is a covered truck with no side windows behind the front seat.

vase

A **vase** is a jar for holding flowers.

vegetable

A **vegetable** is a plant or a part of a plant used for food.

vet

Vet is short for veterinarian. A **vet** is a person who cares for sick animals.

violin

A **violin** is a musical instrument with four strings. A small stick is pulled across the strings to make music.

visit

When you go to see someone, you **visit** them.

vitamin

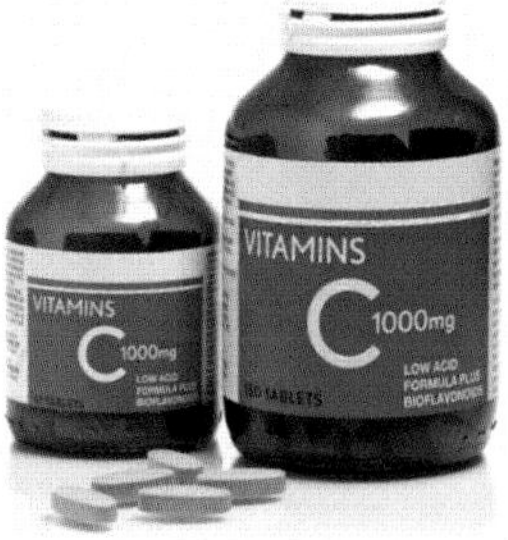

Vitamins help to make your body strong and healthy. They are found in many foods.

voice

You open your mouth and use your **voice** to speak.

volcano

A **volcano** is a mountain from which hot melted rock, gas, steam, and ash from inside the earth sometimes burst.

a b c d e f g h i j k l m n o p q r s t u v w x y z

A B C D E F G H I J K L M N O P Q R S T U V W X Y Z

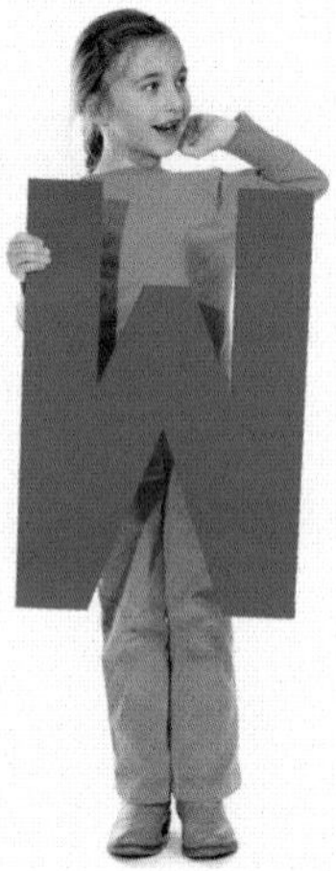

Ww Ww Ww Ww

wake • woke, woken

Wake means to stop sleeping.

wagon

A **wagon** is a four-wheeled vehicle drawn by horses and used to carry loads.

wait

Wait means to stay until someone comes or something happens.

walk

We use our legs and feet to **walk**. We move along by putting one foot in front of the other.

wall

A **wall** is one of the sides of a building or of a room.

want

Want means to feel a desire or a need for something.

warm

Warm is between hot and cold. It's **warm** inside.

wash

When we are dirty, water **washes** us clean.

watch • **watches**

A **watch** is a small clock worn on the wrist.

water

Water is a clear liquid used for drinking, washing, etc.

watering can

A **watering can** is a container with a handle and a long spout used for watering plants.

wave

Wave means to move your hand to say hello or goodbye.

wear • wore, worn

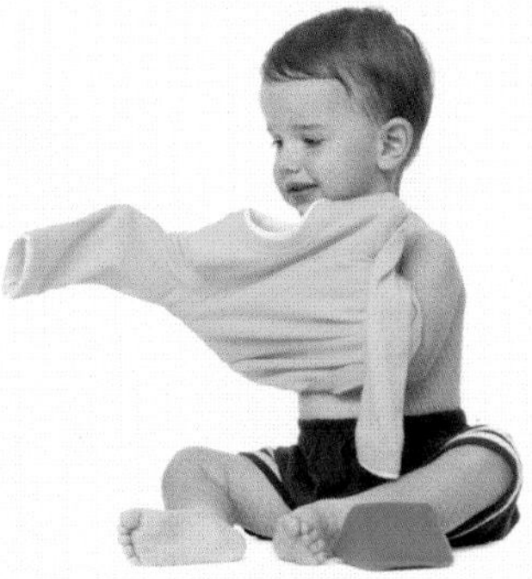

Wear means to have something on your body.

weather

The **weather** is how hot, cold, sunny, or windy it is outside.

week

A **week** has seven days. There are fifty-two **weeks** in a year.

weigh

If you **weigh** something, you find out how heavy it is.

west

The **west** is the place where the sun goes down in the evening.

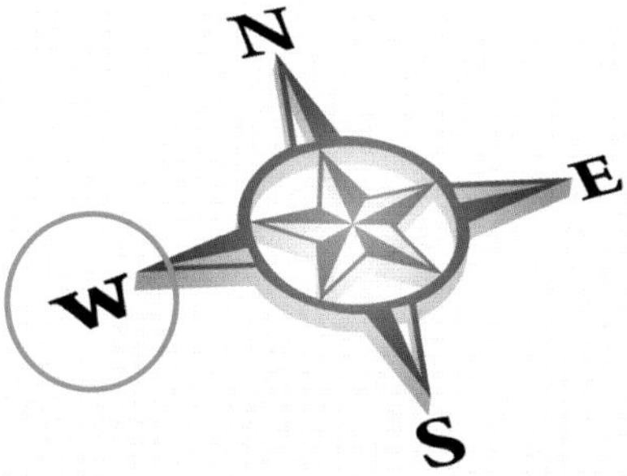

wet

Wet means covered with water.

whale

A **whale** is a very large animal that lives in the sea.

wheel

A **wheel** is a round object that turns when it moves.

wheelbarrow

A **wheelbarrow** is a little cart with one wheel in front and two handles and legs behind. It is used to move things.

wide

Wide means far apart from side to side.

A
B
C
D
E
F
G
H
I
J
K
L
M
N
O
P
Q
R
S
T
U
V
W
X
Y
Z

wife

A **wife** is a woman that a man is married to.

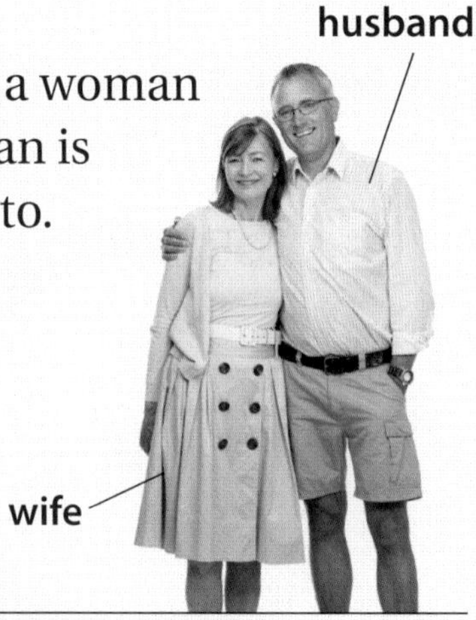

win • won

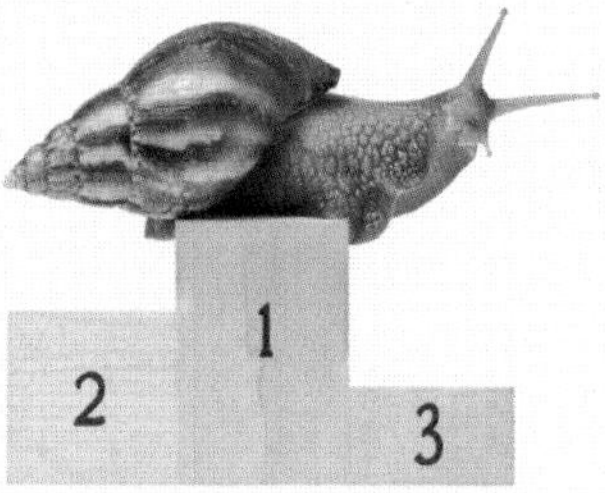

Win means to be the most successful in a game or a race.

wind

The **wind** is air that is moving quickly. Some **winds** are very strong.

windmill

A **windmill** is a machine that uses the force of the wind to push the sails round.

window

A **window** is a sheet of glass on a building for letting in light and air.

wing

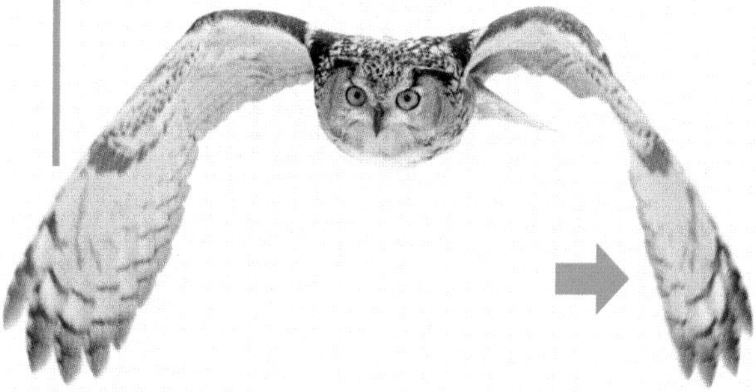

All flying things have **wings** to help them fly. Birds, insects, and airplanes need **wings**.

winter

Winter is a season. It comes after autumn and before spring.

wire

A **wire** is a thread made of metal.

wish

Wish means to want something very much.

witch • **witches**

In fairy tales, a **witch** is a woman with evil magic powers.

without

Without means not having something.

A B C D E F G H I J K L M N O P Q R S T U V W X Y Z

wizard

A **wizard** is a man from legends and stories who has magic powers.

wolf • wolves

A **wolf** is a wild animal that looks like a dog.

woman • women

When a girl grows up, she becomes a **woman.**

wood

Wood is the material that comes from trees. It is used to build or make things.

wool

Wool is sheep's hair. It is spun into yarn and used for making cloth.

work

When someone **works**, they do a job.

world

Everything around us is our **world**. The earth and sky is the **world** in which we live.

worm

A **worm** is a long, thin animal with no legs.

worry • worried

Worry means to keep thinking of bad things that might happen.

wrist

The **wrist** is the joint connecting the arm and the hand.

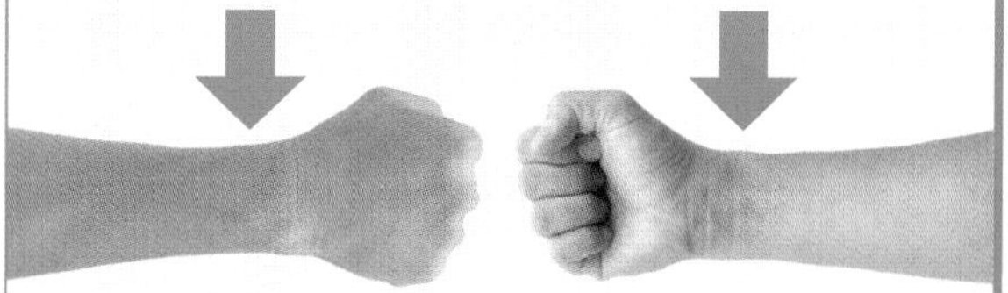

write • wrote, written

When you **write**, you put down words. You could **write** a few words, a letter, a story, or a whole book.

wrong

Something **wrong** is not right or correct.

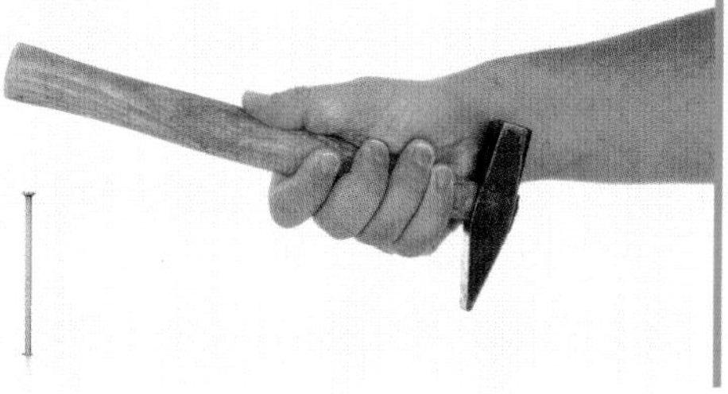

a b c d e f g h i j k l m n o p q r s t u v w x y z

X-ray

An **X-ray** is a kind of picture that shows the inside of the body.

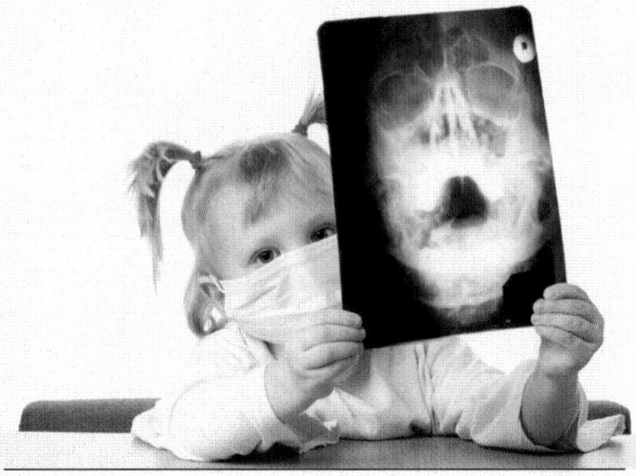

X-mas

X-mas means Christmas.

xylophone

A **xylophone** is a musical instrument. It is made of metal or wooden bars. The bars are different sizes.

yard

A **yard** is an area of land. It is outside a house. Many **yards** are covered with grass.

yacht

A **yacht** is a large ship used for pleasure.

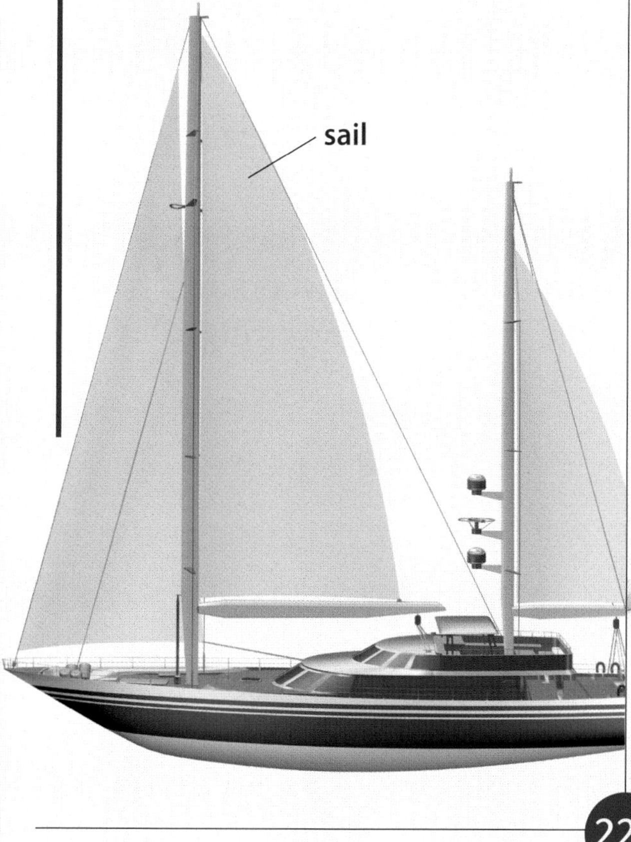

yawn

When you are tired or bored, you open your mouth wide and **yawn**.

year

A **year** is equal to twelve months. Each **year** begins in January and ends in December.

a b c d e f g h i j k l m n o p q r s t u v w x y z

yoga

Yoga is an exercise which includes stretching your body and breathing.

yogurt

Yogurt is a food made from milk which tastes thick and creamy. It often has fruit in it.

yolk

A **yolk** is the yellow part of an egg.

young

When you are **young**, you are not grown-up. Everyone was **young** once!

yo-yo

A **yo-yo** is a toy. It has two round pieces of wood or plastic and a long string.

MFE-D-z

Zz Zz Zz Zz

zebra

A **zebra** is a wild African horse with stripes.

zero

Zero is the number 0. **Zero** means nothing.

zigzag

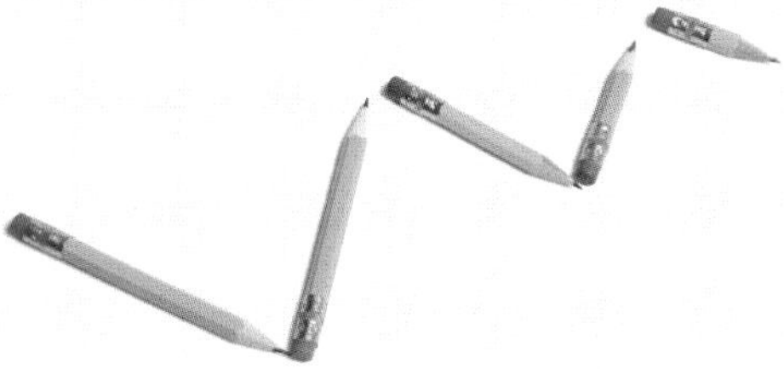

A **zigzag** is a line with sharp angles. If you travel in a **zigzag**, you move suddenly from side to side.

zipper

A **zipper** is used to hold parts of clothes and bags together.

zoo

A **zoo** is a place where wild animals are kept for people to see.

My First
Dictionary

WorldCom Edu Contents Development Team

펴낸이	임 병 업
펴낸곳	(주)월드컴 에듀
등록	2000년 1월 17일
주소	서울특별시 강남구 도곡동 467-6 대림 아크로텔 C동 1403호
전화	02)3273-4300(대표)
팩스	02)3273-4303
홈페이지	www.wcbooks.co.kr
이메일	wc4300@wcbooks.co.kr